HOW TO GROW AMAZING ORGANIC VEGETABLES

HOW TO USE THE 5 FUNDAMENTAL BUILDING BLOCKS OF ORGANIC GARDENING TO SUCCESSFULLY GROW YOUR OWN VEGETABLES

by

K. D. STEWART

CONTENTS

Dedicated to my beautiful wife and three wonderful children, the Bears, whose love and support inspires me to be a better person every day x

A gift just for you

A free fun video with 6 top tips to help you avoid making mistakes when you start growing vegetables.
To access this video just scan the QR code below

INTRODUCTION

"The glory of gardening: hands in the dirt, head in the sun, heart with nature. To nurture a garden is to feed not just the body, but the soul."

— ALFRED AUSTIN

Gardening's always just been a part of life for me. I remember the first time I tasted a store-bought tomato. I was blown away by the lack of flavor. Over the years, mass-produced tomatoes have been bred for a uniform appearance, and as this has happened, one of the genes responsible for storing the sun's energy has been deactivated in the fruit. This gene is still active in the leaves, but 20–30% of a tomato's sugar is produced in the fruit, resulting in a tomato that is far less sweet than one that's grown naturally.

I'd managed to get to the age of eight or nine, I think, before I ever tasted a tomato that had been bred in this way—and that's thanks to my parents.

I grew up in the garden. My parents were avid gardeners. Our garden was my playground, and nearly every fruit and vegetable we had on the dinner table was grown there. One of my favorite jobs in the summer was shelling fava beans (broad beans if you're in the UK). I would sit for hours breathing in the fresh green smell of the pods and listening to the satisfying thud of the beans as I dropped them into the orange plastic bowl my dad always gave me for the job. I loved walking through the cabbage patch with my mom after the rain, picking off snails and slugs and rehoming them somewhere far away from the vegetables. I loved the smell of potatoes pulled from the earth and the sight of the onions hanging in the shed to cure.

It was a way of life, and I never thought to question why we did it, or what the alternative might be. This was long before the word "organic" became a selling point, and I don't remember my parents ever using it. They didn't use chemicals in the garden, but they weren't militant about it —it just wasn't the way they did things.

So when I moved to the UK as a young adult and found myself an allotment, I was taken aback by how many people were using chemical pesticides and herbicides. I just couldn't really see why—the garden I'd grown up in had been a thriving haven of fruit and vegetables, and we'd never needed to resort to using chemical warfare against the slugs.

I lived in a small apartment in East London with no land of its own. Finding an allotment was a top priority for me. If I could avoid living on overpriced and tasteless produce, I was going to make sure I did. Plus, gardening has so much more to offer than the food you produce: I couldn't imagine a life without the fresh air and the feel of dirt beneath my boots. I was lucky enough to find my little patch fairly easily. I think the waiting lists for allotments in London are far longer now. And on that land, I found a way to live the way I'd grown up, while making lifelong friends of other gardeners—many of whom, it turned out, I influenced quite heavily with my own gardening practices.

I didn't go out of my way to teach anyone about organic gardening. I just couldn't understand why anyone would do anything else, so I asked questions, and in return, my fellow gardeners wanted to know what I did instead. Many of them thought that if they didn't use chemicals, their crops wouldn't survive the pests, and their harvests would be less abundant. There were other gardeners on the allotment, of course, who took an organic approach, and from them, I learned techniques I hadn't known about growing up on my parents' land in California.

When I eventually returned to the States, my gardening knowledge was richer than it had ever been, and I had the bug to share my knowledge. Ever since my time in the UK, I've been driven to show reluctant gardeners how easy and effective organic gardening really is—and nine times out of ten, no one really wants to spray their food with chemicals: usually, they just don't see an alternative.

The benefits of organic produce are vast, and in my experience, the only reason people don't want to garden in this way is that they're worried they won't get the results they're looking for. The chances are, that's why you're reading this book. Perhaps you're new to gardening, or perhaps you've been gardening for years and you want to find a way to put that pesticide away for good. Perhaps you have health reasons for wanting to grow organic produce, or perhaps you're just aware of the superior flavor you'll open yourself up to when you do—or maybe you have an inkling that organic is good, but you don't know why. Whatever your reason, you can guarantee that I've come across someone like you before—and I have never met anyone who's failed to produce a fruitful harvest with the methods I grew up around.

The problem I've found with many gardening guides—organic or otherwise—is that they're geared toward either a specifically American market or a specifically British one. Having lived in both countries, I wanted to make sure the book I produced spoke to both audiences. Because the only thing that separates us is the climate we live in and the words we use for our vegetables. The principles of organic gardening are the same wherever you are, so why exclude part of the gardening community?

My aim here is the same as my aim in life: I want to show you that organic gardening is simple, effective, and beneficial—both for you as a gardener, and for the planet as a whole.

So we'll start at the beginning: we'll look at the reasons to grow organically, how to set your garden up for success from the very beginning of your journey, as well as the easiest vegetables to grow when you first start organic gardening. We'll look at pests and disease, of course, because I know that's what you're worried about—but honestly, when you set your garden up the right way, they're far less of a problem than you might imagine. By the time you put this book down, you should have a clear idea of how to approach your first year of organic gardening—and by the time you look back on your garden planner at the end of that year, you should have caught the bug for organic gardening.

I've yet to meet anyone who's gone back to spraying their crops with chemicals. Why would you if you didn't need to?

1

ORGANIC VEGETABLE GARDENING BASICS: THE WHAT AND THE WHY

The secret to organic gardening success begins before you even step outside. I'm not sure that there's anything, actually, where the same key doesn't open the door to success: it's understanding why you're doing what you're doing. So for you, that's understanding why you're going to start an organic garden, and what exactly that looks like.

So let's take a step back for a moment and think about what organic gardening actually is.

WHAT IS ORGANIC GARDENING?

To put it simply, organic gardening requires you to use natural supplies that have been through minimal processes in order to care for your garden. That means no synthetic chemicals and nothing that will contaminate the environment. In organic gardening we treat the soil as the rich ecosystem it is: it's there doing its own thing, and we are merely asking for its help.

In conventional gardening, on the other hand (which I'll use here as a shorthand for non-organic gardening), the soil is viewed as nothing more than a growing medium. Protecting it is not the primary concern, and chemicals are used to achieve the desired results.

In an organic garden, your vegetables are not the only things you're concerned about: to see the best results, you have to view them in the context of the whole ecosystem. Everything on your land has a part to play in that ecosystem and must be respected. The soil you grow in is teeming with life, which is what will support your crops. In return, those crops will give back to the land, providing nutrients and habitats for birds and insects—not all of them are out for your cabbages. This mutually beneficial arrangement creates a perfectly balanced ecosystem that enriches everything you grow.

All gardens would be organic were it not for the creation of synthetic chemicals. The only reason we even have to make a distinction is that we've found a chemical solution to the "problems" presented by gardening.

Nowadays, you probably don't need to take more than 20 steps into a grocery store to see the word "organic" emblazoned on packaging and store signs, but the word didn't come into popular use until midway through the 20th century when sustainable agriculture advocate Jerome Irving Rodale used it in his work to refer to producing food without the use of pesticides.

Now we're used to seeing it everywhere, but the reality is that very few people understand what it really means and why it's good for us.

So let's take a closer look at what it means to grow food organically.

THE FIVE BUILDING BLOCKS OF ORGANIC GARDENING

Organic gardening can be boiled down to five key principles. If we're able to do these things, we have the foundations for a productive and thriving garden that truly meets the requirements of organic gardening.

They are:

- To build and nurture the health of the soil

- To encourage biodiversity in the environment
- To use resources responsibly
- To avoid the use of harmful chemicals
- To maintain and nurture a healthy growing environment

Let's remind ourselves of why we'd want to do that.

WHY GARDEN USING ORGANIC PRINCIPLES?

When someone first asked me this question, I was hard-pressed to find an easy answer.

That's not because there aren't plenty of reasons—I just couldn't fathom why you wouldn't.

Why choose to spray chemicals on something you plan to eat if you don't have to?

Just as the principles of organic gardening are simple, so too are the reasons for practicing it. Put most simply, it's just better: it's better for your health, it's better for the environment, and it's better for the people who live in that environment.

Healthy organic soil is packed full of nutrients and minerals that feed your vegetables, and ultimately, feed you. Organic produce is, therefore, healthier and more nutritious than vegetables that have been produced with the aid of synthetic chemicals. And if you'd like the icing on the cake—you can be sure you won't be ingesting any chemicals either (or bringing them into your home on your shoes and clothes).

The absence of these chemicals also makes your garden a safe haven for birds, bees, and a whole host of other garden critters who we share the land with. Bees are particularly significant here: they're essential pollinators, so making sure they have food and shelter—and a reason to be in our gardens—is beneficial to our crops. By using organic

principles, not only is your garden safer for them, but it's safer for you and your family too—and that becomes particularly important if you have children. Chemicals have been linked to a host of conditions, including cancer and several other chronic diseases... Why expose yourself to them if you don't have to?

While we get sick, the planet gets sick too. But when we nurture healthy soil, using organic principles to guide us, that soil provides a natural storage solution for the carbon in the atmosphere. That carbon does us no good in the atmosphere—it's a major contributing factor to climate change—but in the soil, it feeds our plants and helps to create a healthy and thriving garden. Meanwhile, we're reducing our own contribution to the pollution problem by not adding to the chemicals in the atmosphere.

Ultimately, any chemical you're not buying is a chemical you're not paying for. Organic gardens are cheaper to run. The minimal amount of pest and weed control you'll need to do can be done with homemade solutions and recycled materials.

I don't know of a single gardener who doesn't get pleasure from watching their garden grow. With organic gardening, that pleasure is heightened—at least in my experience. By following the patterns in nature and encouraging the wildlife to do its own thing, you open yourself up to new lessons every day. Nature has a lot to teach the vegetable gardener, and when you don't upset it, it's only too happy to share its lessons.

Of course, the benefits of organic gardening don't stop in the garden. If you're growing vegetables, you're probably growing food you plan to eat—and there are plenty of reasons why you might want that to be organic.

WHY EAT ORGANIC VEGETABLES?

The word "organic" is hot stuff in marketing, and that makes it hard to sift the gold from the dirt when it comes to the actual benefits it brings. That's not to say there aren't plenty of reasons why eating organic is good, it just means you have to look more closely to find information you can trust.

So what do we know about the benefits of eating organic? I've whittled this list down to the benefits that pertain to organic vegetables specifically, but rest assured, if you're a meat-eater, there are plenty of reasons to extend your organic eating to animal products.

Better Flavor

I'm starting here because although the health benefits are important, they often shroud one of the most glorious things about organic produce: the superior flavor. Organic gardening allows produce more time to develop, and the attention paid to soil health results in tastier food. There's nothing more to it than that, but to me, that alone is reason enough to ditch the chemicals.

An All-Round Picture of Good Health

It stands to reason that if you don't ingest harmful chemicals, your health is probably going to benefit. Plus, as we've discussed, the nutrient density of vegetables grown organically is greater thanks to superior soil health, so you'll be feeding your body with everything it needs to maintain good health.

Antioxidant Abundance

You only have to pick up a health article to know that antioxidants are important to human health. They've been shown to be beneficial in the prevention of cancer, heart disease, cognitive decline, vision deterioration, and premature aging. The chemicals used in conventional gardening interfere with the natural organic compounds and the vitamin and mineral content of food, reducing the impact of their antioxidizing properties. Organic produce, on the other hand, provides you with the maximum amount of antioxidants in each serving.

Ingesting Fewer Chemicals

We've touched on this a little already. Links have been made between chemical pesticides and a number of diseases. In addition to those we've already mentioned, they can weaken our immune systems and contribute to headaches and digestive issues. Think back to your school days and the chemistry lab: whenever you add a chemical to something, some kind of reaction is triggered. The same is true of your body—you can't put chemicals into it without triggering a reaction somewhere. This is particularly important for children, who stand to risk more impact on their health when they're still developing.

Ingesting Fewer Toxic Metals

Chemical pesticides aren't the only thing you're welcoming into your body when you eat a conventionally grown carrot. In essence, what you eat comes from the soil. In conventional farming, agrichemicals are used to "improve" the soil; in organic farming, this doesn't happen, so you'll be eating fewer toxic metals. Studies have shown that conventionally grown vegetables contain almost double the amount of cadmium (a naturally occurring toxic metal) of organic vegetables.

Better Immune Health

Mass-produced vegetables grown in the conventional manner are considered "safe" to eat—and by and large, they are. Safe enough, at least. But the long-term consequences of eating food that has been grown with the use of growth hormones and genetic modification are an increased sensitivity to allergens and reduced strength in the immune system. Organic produce, on the other hand, remains unaltered. When you pair this with the higher nutrient density of organic food (which naturally supports immune health), it's clear to see that you can expect to have a stronger immune system when you eat organically.

The benefits of organic gardening are clear, and it's true that once you know what you're doing, it's simpler than many people realize to establish and maintain a thriving organic garden. But I would be setting you up for a fall if I didn't acknowledge that there are challenges you'll face along the way—and some of those challenges are specific to organic gardening.

Take heart in the fact that this is a far shorter list than the list of reasons to use organic techniques—but as we all know, forewarned is forearmed. These aren't reasons not to use organic gardening practices, they're simply things to be aware of before you start.

THE CHALLENGES OF ORGANIC GARDENING

I've highlighted low cost as a benefit, but if you opt for manufactured organic treatments for your garden, you're probably looking at higher costs than you would have with chemical treatments. It's worth mentioning this, but in my opinion, opting for these treatments is unnecessary, so don't let that put you off. Some people say that chemical treatments are more effective than their organic counterparts, but if you use the five building blocks of organic gardening as your guiding stars throughout this process, you're far less likely to need any kind of treatment in the first place.

If you're particularly into perfectly round tomatoes and carrots without twists and knobbles, you may find the aesthetics of organic gardening off-putting. However, even with conventional gardening this can be the case, and I'd hazard a guess that if you're opting to grow your own food, you're probably not wedded to the uniform shapes and sizes you see in the grocery store.

Perhaps the drawback that carries the most weight is the additional time and effort required when you're starting out as an organic gardener. It does require you to put a little more work into understanding the ecosystem of your garden, and you may need a little more time for planning. And to make sure your garden is successful (and less labor-intensive later on), you'll need to put more time into preparing your garden initially than you would with conventional gardening.

To me, that's a small price to pay for the abundance of benefits your organic garden will bring you, but it's worth being aware of any challenge you may face before you begin.

We're going to start with the basics and work up: you're going to understand everything you'll need to do to prepare your garden for success and reduce the risk of disappointing results. That's where the additional time really is worth mentioning—but I promise you, it truly is worth it. If you prepare your garden properly, it will reward you, and throughout the following chapters, you'll learn everything you need to know to do just that.

❖ **Fun Fact:** Organic farms in the USA are allowed to use pesticides. Most synthetic pesticides are prohibited, but some pesticides are classed as "natural," and they're still permitted. So when you buy a bag of carrots carrying the "organic" label, it could have been produced using pesticides made from sulfur, copper, or dairy cultures. More reason to grow your own!

2

YOUR TOOLS: A SMALL BUT ESSENTIAL KIT FOR LONG-TERM GARDENING SUCCESS

We'll start by looking at the basic tools you're going to need to get your garden off the ground. There's actually very little you'll need to get started, and there's no doubt that you'll want to build up your kit as your needs change and your passion grows, but it's wise to start with a few essentials if you want to get off on the right foot. Cutting corners here won't do you any favors: without the right tools, you're going to get frustrated quickly and make simple tasks much harder than they need to be.

I've divided your organic gardening toolbox into three categories: The Essentials (these are the things you really want to make sure you have before you get started); The Extras (the things you don't really need but which will make your life as a gardener more comfortable); and Additional Supplies (these are the things that can't really be described as tools, but which you will need before you start getting your hands dirty).

THE ESSENTIALS

Garden Snips

Odd as it may seem to start with a tool you won't be using until you have plants to look after, a decent pair of snips is one of the most important tools you'll need. A good set of garden snips will help you to harvest delicate fruits and vegetables without harming the plant. Tomatoes, for example, are easy to damage if you pull them off; a pair of snips will make the job easier and protect both your plant and your harvest. What you want to be careful of, however, is that you get the right tool for the job. There are plenty of reasons to have a pair of secateurs at your disposal, but bear in mind that these are designed for pruning thick, woody branches. Snips have sharp pointy blades, and a good pair will be lightweight and spring-loaded.

Ergonomic Shovel

A shovel might seem like a no-brainer, but make it an ergonomic one. You'll spend less effort digging, and it'll take less of a toll on your back. I think it's worth investing in tools that make life easier, and for new gardeners especially, it's advisable to find workarounds for the things that might put you off... hours of back-breaking digging is definitely one of those things.

Hori Hori Knife

It's strange that the hori hori knife is such an unfamiliar concept to new gardeners when it's such a staple once you get started. You may have heard it called a "weeding knife" or a "soil knife," and it's a godsend when it comes to cutting and digging. It's a Japanese tool, and the word "hori" translates as "to dig," but you can also use a hori hori knife for transplanting, pruning, harvesting, and weeding. It has a steel blade with a sharp point at the end and two sharp sides. It's worth spending a bit of money here to get a good one—look for one that comes with a sheath to protect the blade, and a sharpening stone to keep it in peak condition. I have a friend who says he can't afford to buy cheap shoes, and it's worth taking this approach with a hori hori knife too: buy a decent one with a good sheath, look after it well, and you won't need to buy another one.

CobraHead Weeder

We're going to look at how you can build a garden that discourages rampant weed growth, but there's nothing you can do to completely eliminate the weed problem. Your hori hori knife will be your best friend, but it's worth investing in a CobraHead weeder too: the curved head and the long blade are ideal for getting under weeds so you can pull them out from the roots. One of the biggest reasons that weeds come back is that gardeners fail to pull them up properly—it's far too easy to just pull the tops off, which means you aren't actually removing the weed—you're just removing the part you can see. You want to get the whole plant out, roots and all, and a weeding tool like this will help you do just that.

Action Hoe

Also known as a hula hoe, an action hoe is another weeding tool that will cut through weed roots, making them easy to remove with a rake. It's ideal for weeding a large bed before planting and will save you from having to bend over if you have a large space to cover. Look for something lightweight and durable with a comfortable handle.

Bow Rake

To give your seeds the best start in life, you'll need to remove the debris from the earth and level it off, and for that job, you'll need a rake. It'll also help you to spread compost evenly and clean up after the growing season. Look for something strong and durable with steel teeth, but make sure it's lightweight enough to use comfortably. What makes a bow rake stand apart from its cheaper counterpart is that the handle connects to the head at both ends (rather than in the middle), which gives it a better load distribution and extends its lifespan.

Digging Fork

Again, prioritize ergonomics here. Gardening is physically demanding, but there's no sense in making it unnecessarily painful. When you're looking around garden centers, you'll notice that a lot of gardening forks have a D handle, but these aren't the most comfortable option. Look for a radial handle, and choose a lightweight but durable model. The extra money you invest will come back to you in hours saved in preparing your beds—and the chances are, it'll last you longer too.

Hose and Sprayer

Watering your garden is going to be a regular task, especially when your seedlings are young as you'll need to be hand watering once or twice a day. That makes a garden hose an essential piece of kit, but you'll want a sprayer nozzle too so you don't overwhelm young plants with heavy streams of water. The best option is to choose a nozzle with several jet options—that way, you can use a fine mist setting for younger and more delicate plants, but you'll have the option of a stronger jet for bigger plants.

Soil Thermometer

We'll talk about soil temperature a lot throughout this book: understanding it is key to giving your plants their best chance in life. There are various kinds of thermometers that you can get, some sport a digital display so you can read them while they're still in the soil, and others are modeled on the conventional thermometer, meaning you'll have to pull them out of the soil to read the temperature. It really doesn't matter what type you choose, you simply need something that will allow you to check the conditions easily and accurately so that you know when it's time to plant different crops.

Wheelbarrow

Wheeled carts for transporting earth and rocks around the garden are nearly always called wheelbarrows in the UK, but you might hear of them called yard cards in the US, too. A basic wheelbarrow is all you really need, but you can get multi-functional carts if you want to up your game. Some high-end models will fold flat and double up as a bench, and some have separate compartments for storing or carrying different things. Whatever you choose, make sure it has a good weight distribution so it's easy to wheel around and will do most of the back work for you.

Gardening Gloves

Don't make the mistake of thinking gardening gloves are an optional extra: you'd be surprised by how easy it is to get cuts and nicks, and you may even find that some plants cause skin irritation. It's not worth looking at the cheap ones in the bargain bin though—they won't last, and thorns will go through them easily. Forestry gloves made from silicone and lightweight fabric are a good option: essentially, you want something thick and durable, but also light and breathable.

THE EXTRAS

Kneeling Pad

Let's be honest, you don't need a kneeling pad. People have been kneeling on the ground for centuries, and unless you have a medical issue with your knees, it's not going to cause you any major damage. That said, kneeling and squatting can be uncomfortable, and there'll always be that one pebble you didn't notice waiting to attack, so a durable foam kneeling pad isn't a bad investment. If you're going to get one, choose a pad that's a minimum of 1-inch thick.

Gardening Apron

You definitely don't need a gardening apron, and some gardeners actively dislike them. For many people, wearing old clothes that you don't mind dirtying is enough, and some people don't like the extra fabric getting in the way. For others, though, a gardening apron is a good way of keeping several tools on you at once without having to walk up and down the garden for supplies. If you do decide to invest in a gardening apron, check the depth of the pockets: you want to be able to fit all your small tools in there, as well as your seeds, and maybe a roll of garden twine.

Garden Colander

I almost feel ridiculous including this: you can collect your harvest in anything you like, after all. But I love my garden colander so much, it would be remiss not to mention it. What's great about them is that you can give your harvest a quick rinse with the hose before you take it indoors, getting rid of excess dirt and bugs before you get to the sink. It just makes everything a lot cleaner and neater.

Heat Mats

They're certainly not essential, but if you're going to be starting plants from seed, heat mats aren't a bad idea. Seeds can be particular about the soil temperature, and for those that need warmer soil, a heat mat can encourage germination. That said, simply keeping your seed trays in a greenhouse or in front of a sunny window will be sufficient, so unless you have trouble finding a consistently warm spot, you don't really need them, and not using them will allow you to use less energy.

ADDITIONAL SUPPLIES

Starter Mixes

Starter mixes are soil mixtures designed to give your seeds the best start in life. They tend to be lighter than standard potting soil, with finer particles that make it easier for roots to develop. That said, they're not always made of soil: seedlings get their nutrients from the seed at the beginning of their life, so they don't rely on soil to nourish them. Some starter mixes, therefore, are made solely from coconut coir, and they're a good option if you want to ensure a contaminant-free mix. You can get sterilized seed mixes, which are still OK for organic gardening, as they're treated using heat rather than chemicals to get rid of pathogens.

You want a lightweight starter mix that retains water, so the things to look out for are moss or coconut coir (these help with water retention) and perlite or vermiculite (these provide aeration). Coconut coir is generally considered the more sustainable option, but what about Peat? Bear in mind that it's not considered best practice to use peat in organic gardening, as its extraction causes the destruction of a natural habitat, and no level of management will completely solve this problem. Both perlite and vermiculite are approved for organic gardening, but they may undergo processes, so check the labeling on your mix to be sure you've chosen an organic option.

A good starter mix also contains diatomaceous earth, which is composed of fossilized plants. It naturally destroys any bugs that might threaten your seedlings, giving them the best chance of successful germination.

Most seedlings like an acidic pH level, so look for a starter mix with a pH level of 5.5–6.5.

Any starter mix that has been certified organic will be a good choice, but if you're overwhelmed by the options, I've had good success with Epsoma's Organic Seed Starter Premium Potting Mix.

Compost

For organic gardening, good-quality compost is an absolute must. We'll look at building your own in Chapter 3, which, ultimately, is what I'd recommend, but you can also buy it from your garden center. Just check that it's safe for vegetable gardening and has been certified organic before you buy. Compost is simply the natural result of decayed organic matter (grass clippings, leaves, vegetable trimmings, animal manure, etc.). It's filled with moisture and nutrients to feed your plants, and packed full of microorganisms, worms, and helpful insects. You only really need to buy it if you're in short supply, and possibly at the beginning of your vegetable gardening journey when you haven't had a chance to build your own stash.

Mulch

Mulch is used to hold moisture in the ground and reduce weeds. Make sure you choose a mulch designed for organic vegetable gardening though: in landscaping, wood chips are

used, and this is also known as mulch, but it isn't what you want for growing food. You want mulch made from organic matter that will nourish your soil as it breaks down over time.

Organic Fertilizer

Maintain a healthy organic garden for long enough, and you probably won't have much use for fertilizer, as you'll have built a strong, nutrient-rich soil for your plants. This takes time, however, so at the beginning of your journey, your seedlings may need a little extra boost. The key nutrients you're looking for in a fertilizer are nitrogen, phosphorus, and potassium, and you'll know these are present if the label says "NPK." Look for a well-balanced fertilizer containing both these key nutrients as well as a good range of micronutrients—and of course, make sure it's certified organic.

Kelp-based fertilizers are a good option—or just straight up kelp with nothing added. It contains potassium and nitrogen naturally and has the added bonus of stimulating soil development. Alfalfa meal is another good option, containing all three key nutrients and improving soil quality. Cow manure and chicken manure can also be used, but if you're a beginner gardener, these can be intimidating options, so only use them if you're comfortable, and you're confident that the animals were fed an organic diet.

If you're looking for a quick solution to pick up at the garden center, I'd recommend Jobe's Organics All Purpose Granular Plant Food, which contains NPK at a ratio of 4–4–4. It's a good allrounder, and you can use it all over your garden if you just want to buy one product. Read the packaging for directions of how much to apply, and you won't go wrong.

Support Structures

These are essential if you're growing vining or tall plants. It's worth deciding on what you'll be planting before making an investment, however: exactly what support you need will depend on what you're growing. You may need trellising, stakes, or cages, and you may not need all of them, so wait until you have a plan ready before you decide what to buy. Your seed packets will tell you what you can expect from your plants, and that will tell you what supports you need. Really, you don't need to invest in support structures at the very beginning, but I've included them here because you'll need them eventually, and it's better to be prepared now.

Containers and Planters

These are only essential if you're planning on planting in pots—but if you are, you need to be well-prepared from the outset. You can make almost any container into a plant pot, but I would go for practicality over style. You'll need to consider capacity (based on the size of your plants at maturity), and broadly speaking, you want a container that holds water well. Terra cotta is pretty, but bear in mind that terra cotta pots dry out quickly (especially small ones); metal is good at holding water, but it's not ideal in hot weather as it absorbs heat. Personally, I prefer plastic pots for vegetables, but be mindful of the fact that plastic can break down over time and affect the soil quality. Look at the recycling codes on the bottom to avoid this: 1, 2, 4, and 5 indicate that the plastic has been approved for storing food. You can also get more sustainable pots made from compostable materials. Whatever containers you buy, make sure they have drainage holes in the bottom. If they don't, you'll need to drill your own.

Row Covers

Seedlings are delicate little things, and they need protection from weather, birds, and insects. Row covers are the easiest way to do this, and they're easy to find in the garden center. Look for UV-resistant materials and good ventilation, all of which will be clearly marked on the packaging.

Netting

Netting is an extra layer of protection, and can even be used once your plants are mature. It's not necessarily essential, but if you have larger visitors to your garden like rabbits or deer, netting will keep your crops safe from theft.

Burlap

Burlap is biodegradable and quite cheap, and it's worth having on hand from the beginning. It's a great quick-fix option for protecting your plants if the temperature suddenly plummets, and it will also protect your plants from pests. As an added bonus, you can use it for germinating seeds (it heats up the soil and speeds up germination).

Twine

You'll need twine in your garden at some point, so add it to your tool kit before you start. If you're growing tomatoes, it'll come in handy for tying them to stakes, but it's useful for general control and tidiness. Any time you have vines sprawling over your garden or tall plants drooping away from their support structures, twine will be your answer. I'd recommend using a hemp twine—it's completely natural and very easy to use.

LET'S TALK GREENHOUSES

I could probably write a whole book about greenhouses, so I'm not going to go into a ton of detail here. However, if you have space for one, it's a worthwhile investment, so it's worth having a quick look before we move on. Don't panic if you don't have the space or the money for a greenhouse though: it's perfectly possible to nurture a thriving garden without one.

The Benefits of a Greenhouse

What a greenhouse essentially gives you is an opportunity for year-round growing. It's a space where you can control the temperature, maintaining a good climate for healthy growth even when the weather has its own ideas. You can also control irrigation to a greater degree than you can outside, and this means you can cultivate an ideal humidity level for growing. Through the strategic positioning of shelves and covers, you also gain total control over the amount of light and shade different plants get, allowing you to grow a variety of plants with different light needs. A greenhouse is the perfect place for starting seeds and keeping young seedlings until the temperature outside is warm enough for them to thrive. Tomatoes, in particular, are sensitive to frost and must be kept inside until after the last frost date. If you have a greenhouse, this is much easier to do if you want to keep your living room free of plants.

Greenhouse Kits

If you decide a greenhouse would be a good addition to your garden, a greenhouse kit is probably your easiest route. You essentially have two options: attached or freestanding.

An attached greenhouse uses an existing wall of your house or garage to bear most of the weight, with the other three sides being lighter. This is a cheaper option and a good choice for growing seedlings and herbs. The only real drawback is that the use of an existing wall means you'll only be getting sunlight through three walls.

A freestanding greenhouse, meanwhile, can be erected on any level area of your garden, so long as it gets plenty of light. It's a more expensive option than an attached greenhouse, but you can grow a diverse range of plants inside them, so it's worth the extra money. In most regions, a freestanding greenhouse will mean you can start planting much earlier in the year and bring your plants inside to extend the growing season after the first frost.

Whether you choose a freestanding or an attached design, glazing is key: it's what protects your plants from the weather while letting light and heat in. Glass is the best option, but it isn't cheap. Plastic sheeting is a budget-friendly alternative, but it doesn't last as long. A good middle option is polycarbonate, which is cheaper than glass and is actually better at retaining heat. It's durable and lightweight and has the advantage of fitting both flat and curved surfaces.

Choosing a Location

You will need level ground with as much sun exposure as possible—ideally a minimum of 6 hours a day in the winter. If you set it up east to west, the biggest side will get full sun from the south. If you live in a place where this isn't possible, however, you can also install grow lights to make up for it.

You'll also have to think about the tree coverage: some shade in the summer is useful, but during the winter, you want to avoid the shadows of coniferous trees that don't lose their leaves. Positioning your greenhouse near deciduous trees will give you a happy balance of shade during the summer and light during the winter.

It's also worth considering your utilities: you need to be able to access water at the very least, but you'll also need electricity if you're using grow lights or installing heating systems. Make sure you can access these from your greenhouse location.

As for the surface, your main aim is good drainage, but beyond that, as long as it's level, the details don't matter too much. Lay landscape cloth to discourage weeds, and cover it with a 3-inch layer of gravel before you put the greenhouse together.

Controlling the Environment

Since the whole idea of a greenhouse is to create the optimum growing environment, you need to get this right, and what you need to do to create the ideal conditions will depend on your location and climate. If you live in a colder area, insulation may be necessary: even with good sun exposure, an uninsulated structure will lose a lot of heat at night. You may want to consider a solar or electric heater in this case. You can also hang heat lamps over the plants. Just make sure you have sufficient ventilation and an automatic shut-off system for safety.

For an all-natural heating system, try putting rocks or water containers in the greenhouse: these will harvest heat from the sun during the day and help the structure stay warm overnight. I do this in my own greenhouse during the winter, and it never fails to amaze me how much of a difference it makes.

On the other hand, if you live in a hot region, reducing the temperature will be your priority, in which case, look to shading options. You can shade your plants with polypropylene cloth, vinyl shading, or wooden screens.

Regardless of your climate, ventilation will be important. The simplest solution is to open windows and manual vents, but you can also get electric vents that will open automatically when the temperature rises. You could also install a fan to keep up airflow. Bear in mind, however, that one of the key principles of organic gardening is to use resources responsibly. Therefore, the less energy you can use to run your garden, the better.

DIY Alternatives

If you like the benefits a greenhouse brings but don't have the budget or space, you can always consider DIY solutions. There are probably hundreds of things you could do to emulate greenhouse conditions, and when I had my allotment, I saw people doing all kinds of things. I think my favorite was the umbrella greenhouse: nothing more complicated than a transparent dome umbrella with the handle cut down and secured in the ground, with the plastic covering the plants.

I've also seen CD-case greenhouses, greenhouses fashioned out of plastic bottles, and pallet greenhouses. Just google creative ideas for DIY greenhouses and you're sure to find something that speaks to you. The aim is to control the temperature and light: as long as you do this, you can't go far wrong.

❖**Fun Fact:** Like most great inventions, the greenhouse can be dated back to the Romans. The first known greenhouse was created around 30 A.D. to supply Emperor Tiberius with a year-round supply of cucumbers, which he was recommended to eat regularly for good health.

3

STEP 1: PREPARING YOUR GROWING AREA FOR A THRIVING GARDEN

You know why you're doing this, and you have your tools. Now it's time to get started, and that means taking the long view. A thriving organic garden starts with the soil, and in my experience, it's the gardeners who don't understand this who run into the most problems. At

no point on this journey are we feeding the vegetables: we are feeding the soil, and that's what will promote healthy growth. For as long as you have a vegetable garden, you will be working with the natural life of the soil rather than viewing it simply as a medium for growing your food: look after it, and it will look after you.

Healthy soil is teeming with life and packed full of nutrients. Think back to the building blocks of organic gardening we looked at in Chapter 1. To make sure your soil is fertile, we need to zone in on two of those points: building and maintaining soil health, and encouraging biodiversity.

There are four main ways to make sure this happens: through the use of compost to add nutrients and build a solid structure to support the roots of your plants; through minimal digging so you don't disturb the life of the soil; through planning what you're going to plant to minimize disease and pests; and through growing particular plants to develop the composition of the soil and minimize weed growth. That's not to say you can't grow any vegetable you like—but that will only be possible when we give the soil its best chance to help us.

Understanding and Improving Your Soil

It doesn't help to rush into organic gardening, and before you can begin building rich and fertile soil, you will need to get to know what you're working with. The first step, therefore, is to investigate the soil you already have in your garden. A soil testing kit will help you here. You can easily get hold of one online or from your garden center, and it will give you a good idea of the profile of your soil: you'll be able to measure the nutrients in the soil, its pH level, and its composition. You'll also be able to tell a certain amount simply by getting your hands dirty—is it, for example, heavy and damp, or is it light and sandy? This simple exercise will tell you how much water it holds. Once you know what it is you're working with, you can take steps to improve it.

There are two ways you can improve your soil for organic gardening: through the use of compost and manure; and by adding topsoil.

Compost and Manure

Making your own compost and adding manure are probably the best ways to improve your soil, and unlike commercial fertilizers, they will improve the structure of your soil as well as

its nutrient content. It stands to reason: compost and manure are examples of natural waste, and adding them to your garden will encourage your soil to reuse nutrients just as it does in nature. As waste begins to rot, it naturally kills off harmful bacteria, simultaneously hampering weed growth and feeding the life in the soil. The composting process is varied, and can take as little as 6 weeks and as long as a year, depending on the materials being broken down.

We'll look at how you can make your own compost a little later in the chapter, but first, let's look a little more closely at what it's made up of.

Plant Waste

Think of plant waste as soil food. Everything from grass trimmings to vegetable waste counts, but it's important to compost it before adding it to the garden (this makes sure any diseases are destroyed).

There are also a few considerations you'll have to make to ensure that the compost you use is truly organic. Ideally, you want to avoid using peat for the reasons we touched on in Chapter 2. You should also be mindful of using leaf waste that has been sourced from woodlands, as this is removing resources from another ecosystem. Lastly, be careful not to use any material that may be contaminated by toxins—using grass cuttings from a local park, for example, is a risky business because you don't know what chemicals may have been used for weed and pest control. The more waste you can collect from your own ecosystem, the better it is from an organic point of view, and the more you can trust what it will add to your garden. That said, if you're able to source plant waste from certified organic sources where removing it will not be taking away from another ecosystem, go for it.

Animal Waste

Unless you already keep livestock, you're unlikely to be able to source animal waste from your own environment. However, if you're comfortable with the idea and able to get hold of an organic source, it can do wonders to improve your soil. Your best option is straw-based manure from an organic farm. It should have been rotting down for a minimum of 6 months before you use it so that harmful pathogens have been destroyed.

I wouldn't attempt to obtain animal waste from anywhere other than an organic farm, but if you do, bear in mind that you must avoid human waste or waste from domestic animals, as well as chemical-based compost activators.

Topsoil

Topsoil, unsurprisingly, is the highly nutritious top layer of soil, which you may need to buy when you're starting your garden if you have poor soil. This is easy to come by in garden centers—just make sure it's been certified organic.

Potting Mix

We discussed starter mixes in Chapter 2, but if you'll be growing in containers, you'll need a potting mix for these too, and it will need to have a higher nutrient content than your starter mix. Ideally, you'll make your own potting mix from soil and compost, but this isn't possible in every garden. If you need to buy it pre-mixed, opt for a peat-free mix, and check that it's been certified organic.

If you're growing in containers, you could also consider using a liquid feed, which will enrich the soil with nutrients, but is generally more effective in restricted environments. You can make your own using plant waste, or you can buy a commercial product with an organic certification.

Fertilizers

If your soil is healthy enough to support plant life on its own, you can avoid using fertilizers at all. Your compost will do far more good than a liquid or granular fertilizer can, as these products can only boost the nutrient value of the soil, and will do nothing to improve structure. However, when you're starting out it can be helpful to give your soil an extra boost—a bit like taking vitamin supplements to support a healthy diet. For organic gardening, you'll need a fertilizer composed of minerals, plant waste, or animal waste. Again, check that whatever you buy has been certified organic.

An alternative to buying fertilizer is to dig in nettles and other leaves or add them as mulch.

You could also use wood ash, as long as it hasn't been treated with chemicals.

Encouraging Biodiversity

With soil improvement in hand, your next step is to encourage biodiversity, which will feed the soil and promote natural fertility and structure. Biodiversity simply means the presence of different forms of life, and there are three central ways you can encourage this: you can grow a range of different plants; you can provide local wildlife with food and a habitat; and you can continue to feed the life in your soil. With all three bases covered, you will establish an environment with good biodiversity, including flora, fauna, and beneficial microbes and bacteria. Each component will work together to create a balanced, harmonious environment in which you can grow healthy crops with minimal risk of pests and disease.

By creating rich and fertile soil, you've already taken a huge step toward encouraging biodiversity. What else you're able to do largely depends on the size of the space you're working with. Ideally, you want to grow flowers and shrubs as well as vegetables, which will provide birds and insects with food and encourage them to shelter. Try not to be too regimented in your garden layout: if you can, let the grass grow longer in some areas, and allow leaves to build up under the hedge. Areas like this provide welcome shelter to local wildlife.

Feed the birds, build a pond, grow flowers to encourage pollinators... The more biodiversity you can create in your garden, the better it will be for your vegetables. Think of your garden as an organic garden first and a vegetable garden second—this is how you will get the best results in your produce.

Making Your Own Compost

By now, you know how crucial compost is for your garden, so let's take a closer look at how you can make your own. What you're aiming to create is a dark and crumbly mixture that is rich in nutrients and sweet in smell. If you don't already make your own compost, you stand to reduce your contribution to landfill waste by up to 40%, so you'll be benefiting the environment as well as your garden.

The first thing you'll need is a compost bin. You could just use a covered heap, but personally, I think a bin is easier to manage. You can easily build your own if you're the DIY type, or you can buy one. The only requirements are that it has a lid, has no gaps down the side, and is easy to access. Ideally, you want to keep it in a sunny area of the garden directly on top of the soil and away from water.

Compost Ingredients

You can essentially compost anything that once lived, but you should avoid anything that might attract rats and mice, so no cooked food, meat, or dairy products should make it into your compost bin. A good compost is a balanced mixture of green and brown waste, as the two types rot at different paces and ensure a healthy mix of nutrients. Green waste is rich in nitrogen, while brown waste has a high carbon content, and the secret is to balance the two.

Green Waste

Green waste is easy to spot because it is, broadly speaking, green. It might include young weeds, grass trimmings, nettle leaves and stems, and soft green trimmings from hedges and trees. Also included in this category are raw fruit and vegetable peelings, coffee grounds and tea leaves, and animal and poultry manure (from herbivores only).

Brown Waste

In the brown waste category, you have straw, cardboard, pet bedding, woody hedge trimmings, waste paper, kitchen paper, and old plants. Brown waste will decompose more slowly, so make sure it's chopped up before adding it to your compost bin.

Other Items

There are a few additional things you can add to your compost that don't fit neatly in either category. Small amounts of wood ash are fine to add, as are eggshells, hair clippings, and natural fibers like cotton and wool.

How to Make Compost

At the basic level, all you really need to do is add your ingredients to your bin, and they will break down over time. However, for the most balanced and nutritious mix, the ideal approach is to include equal amounts of green waste and brown waste. There are three ways you can do this: the hot heap method, the cool heap method, and a hybrid approach.

Hot Heap Method

This takes a bit more time, but it produces results more quickly. You want to gather together enough waste to fill your bin straight away, mixing it several times first to encourage airflow. As you fill the container, add water at regular intervals. After a few days, the contents of your bin will warm up, cooling again a couple of weeks later. This indicates that it's time to mix up the contents again. The best way to do this is to remove everything from the bin. If the mixture is very dry, add more water; if it's soggy, add more waste. After it has been thoroughly mixed, return the contents to the bin. The mixture may heat up again at this stage. You can repeat the process to ensure more oxygen reaches the microbes breaking down the waste. Once you notice that your compost heap isn't heating up anymore, leave it alone while the composting process finishes.

Cool Heap Method

This approach is less labor-intensive, but it'll take longer for the waste to decompose. Try to collect enough waste to get a 12-inch layer into your compost bin the first time you add to it. Try to ensure that there is an equal amount of bulky brown waste in with your green waste, as this will create space for air. Once your first layer is in place, continue to fill your compost bin as waste arises, being mindful of balance. It's highly likely that you'll never fill the whole container, but if you do, stop adding to the pile. Once it has finished composting, it's ready to use, but this could take a full year. Use the lower layers first, and mix everything left behind to restore balance. As with the hot heap method, add water to a dry compost bin and dry waste if it is too wet.

A Hybrid Approach

You can combine the hot heap and the cool heap method by filling your bin as you acquire waste (cool method) and mixing it when you can (hot method). Mixing will increase the heat, speeding up decomposition, so the more you mix, the quicker you'll have usable compost.

Recognizing When Your Compost Is Ready

Generally, it will be about a year before a compost pile is ready for use, but it can be done in as little as 2 months. The more work you do to mix it, the quicker you'll see results. You'll know you have usable compost when it has turned dark brown and crumbly, and smells sweet and earthy. Don't worry too much if it's lumpy or sticky though. It can still be used, and any big bits that haven't yet decomposed can be added back to the bin.

Extra Tips for Successful Compost

For superior compost, there are a few ways to refine the contents of your bin.

Grass Clippings: Mix these up with brown waste to avoid slime.

Autumn Leaves: You can add these to your compost bin directly, but you'd be better off making leaf mold. To do this, pack bin bags with wet leaves, and leave for a year before using.

Weeds and Weed Seeds: If you're using the hot heap method, some perennial weeds won't survive, but to be on the safe side avoid the most persistent ones like ground elder and celandines. Instead, add them to a bin bag with lawn trimmings and leave the bag closed for a few months before adding the contents to your compost bin. Weed seeds should be killed in a hot heap but might survive a cool heap. If you notice weeds growing in your compost, avoid spreading it on top of the soil, and instead, dig it in.

Diseased Plants: If you have a plant with a soil-borne disease, keep it out of the compost bin. Other diseased plants will be OK in a hot heap, but may not be safe in a cool heap. I'd recommend leaving all diseased plants out of your compost to be on the safe side.

Hedge Trimmings: Always chop these up before adding them to your compost bin and mix them well with green waste. Tread down the pile if possible, and keep it covered.

Paper and Cardboard: Small amounts of paper are fine, but if you have a lot send it to recycling instead. Cardboard and kitchen paper, however, are great for balancing out green waste, so add this freely, scrunching it up first.

Wood and Sawdust: While technically compostable, these items are slow to decay and can monopolize nitrogen.

Add them only in small quantities with plenty of green waste, and don't use them unless you know they haven't been chemically treated.

Animal Manure: On the whole, this shouldn't come from domestic animals, but if you have small pets like guinea pigs or hamsters, their straw and bedding waste will be fine to use, even if there are a few droppings in there.

Preparing Your Growing Area: Step by Step

With a comprehensive understanding of soil improvement and the need for biodiversity in your garden, you're ready to prepare your growing area. Essentially, this simply involves removing the weeds and applying the soil improvement techniques you've already learned.

Step 1: Plot Division

If you have a large area and a lot of weeds to deal with, begin by dividing your plot in half. One half you will be digging up to remove weeds, and the other you will be feeding with mulch to suppress their growth.

Step 2: Weed Removal

Dig over the area you want to start planting, removing woody weeds and brambles from the root. Compost everything you can, but remember to leave weed roots out of your compost bin (you can drown these in water instead, and compost them after a couple of months).

Step 3: Mulching

On the other half of your plot, cut down weed leaves to just higher than the level of the soil, and then cover with mulch to deprive them of light. You can use compost, or you can buy an organic mulch. You'll need to leave this alone for 6–12 months, letting nature take its course to enrich the soil.

Step 4: Digging and Soil Improvement

On the half of your plot that you dug the weeds out of, dig compost into the top 4 inches of soil. You don't need to be too precise, but I'd go for around one wheelbarrow full of compost for every 50 square feet. From here, if you're going to sow seeds, break up the topsoil with your rake to give your seeds their best chance of germinating.

If you'll be planting in containers, prepare your potting mix as we discussed earlier and fill your containers.

❖ **Fun Fact:** Did you know that in one teaspoon of soil, you'll find more microorganisms than the number of people on Earth?

4

STEP 2: BUILDING ON SUCCESS: PLANNING YOUR PLANTING

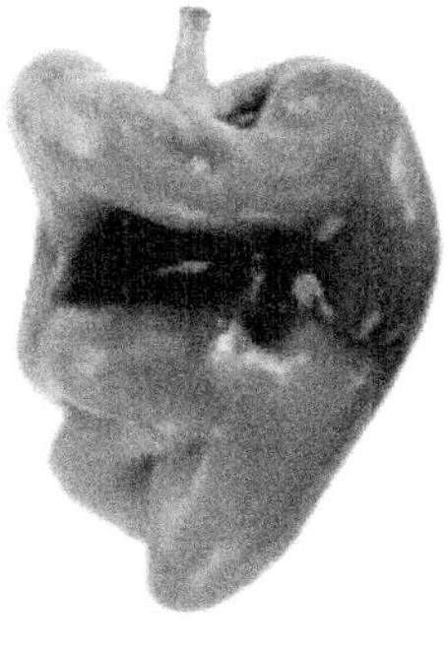

You may remember me mentioning at the beginning of the last chapter that planning your planting is a key way to support soil health, and now that you've prepared your growing area, you'll want to do everything in your power to do this. We'll start by looking at the value of crop rotation, and then we'll take a closer look at how you can plan your vegetable garden.

A quick note before we begin: Throughout the rest of the book, I'll base my examples on a climate akin to Hardiness Zone H7 in the UK and USDA Zone 5 in the USA. Be aware that if you live in a different climate, you'll want to make adjustments for your own growing region (see Chapter 11 for more details on how to do this).

THE VALUE OF CROP ROTATION IN ORGANIC GARDENING

Crop rotation simply refers to the practice of planting a different set of crops in a given area each growing season. Changing where your vegetables are planted each year is a simple way to nourish your soil and maintain a thriving growing area. By planting root vegetables like carrots in one area, you allow the soil to open up making a good spot for crops with shallow roots the following year—this helps you to build a good soil structure. This approach also helps you make efficient use of your compost, as the different nutrient requirements of the vegetables means that you can concentrate your "feeding" on one area. It also gives you greater control over weed invasions and helps to prevent disease, which can build up in the soil if one type of plant is continuously grown in the same space.

Personally, I prefer a yearly rotation, but if you wanted, you could easily rotate over several years. In my opinion, however, an annual rotation helps you keep on top of things and keeps things fresh from year to year.

To keep crop rotation simple, I'd advise a simple 3-step approach:

1. Divide your plot into sections (how many will depend on the size of your growing area and the variety of crops you want to grow).
2. Group your vegetables by family.
3. Move each family to a different section of your growing area each year. This makes planning a bit more straightforward because you don't need to plan a separate location for every single crop—you can simply move the whole family to a new area.

A Quick Guide to Vegetable Families

Family	Vegetables
Legumes	Peas, all varieties of bean
Roots	Carrots, beetroot, celery, celeriac, parsnips, fennel
Cucurbitaceae (Gourds)	Cucumbers, zucchini (courgettes, UK), squash, pumpkins
Brassicas	Cabbages, cauliflowers, broccoli, Brussels sprouts, rutabaga (swedes, UK) turnips, kale, radishes, greens
Solanaceae	Tomatoes, potatoes, peppers, eggplant (aubergines, UK)
Alliums	Onions, shallots, garlic, leeks

PLANNING YOUR GARDEN

I became particularly adept at planning when I lived in the UK, where the seasons are distinct and the climate is wildly different throughout the year. Planning is a good idea wherever you live, however, not only to maintain a constant supply of vegetables but also to make sure the soil is supported throughout the year.

To me, "planning" doesn't just refer to deciding what you're going to plant—it also extends to deciding when to plant, accounting for empty spaces, and extending the growing season, all of which we'll look at more closely here.

Planning What to Grow

The best way to approach this is to look at the year as a whole and plan to keep your garden providing you with food throughout the whole year. I've broken this down by season, but do remember to adjust for your own growing region. Your seed packets will tell you exactly what can be harvested when. I'd recommend making yourself a chart similar to the one below, replacing my notes with the vegetables you'd most like to grow.

Season	Vegetables to Be Harvested
Spring	There's little to be harvested at this time, but if you plan for the other seasons well, you will be able to store enough to keep you in produce during the planting season.
Summer	Most of your vegetables will be harvested during the summer, and some (like beans and peas) can be dried for the fall and winter.
Fall (Autumn, UK)	Roots like carrots and beetroot can be harvested and stored during the fall, and pumpkins and squash can be harvested in late fall and stored for the rest of the year.
Winter	Cabbages, turnips, broccoli, and kale will all grow through the colder months, as will some spinach beets. Parsnips actually develop in flavor if they're not harvested until after the first frost, and will store well through the winter.

Planning to Sow

Planning your sowing essentially means you can achieve a succession of crops by transplanting a few seedlings every few weeks.

To make sure you have greens in at the beginning of spring, you want to sow quick-germinating seeds like salad leaves indoors early: if you have a greenhouse, you're sorted, but even if you don't, a bright windowsill in January and February will be fine. Some herbs, including parsley and cilantro (coriander, UK), will be fine here too.

If you take this approach, I'd recommend using a module tray as the compartments allow for deeper soil than standard seed trays, allowing your plants more chance to extend their roots. This, in turn, will give you greater flexibility, and you can delay planting outdoors if the weather isn't onside.

Once you do transplant your seedlings, plant up another batch. This succession approach will mean you'll have a constant supply of food instead of one large harvest.

It's commonly believed that you should stop sowing once summer arrives, but that's not your best plan if you want to continue harvesting throughout the fall. Continue sowing as late as you can to make the most of growing time.

Carrots are a good example here: you can sow them in June to use throughout the winter, but you can also sow another batch as late as August, as long as you choose an "early" variety that doesn't require as long to mature.

Planning for Gaps

Again, your best bet is to look at the seed packets and make yourself a simple chart, aiming to sow in succession and for as long as possible. However, a word of caution: You'll need to be careful that you choose the right variety. Early varieties reach maturity more quickly, so they're good to use at the beginning and end of the season. Mini varieties are also a good bet: they'll be ready more quickly and can fill gaps in the harvest season.

You can also plan to harvest some of your crops early. This gives you the advantage of avoiding a glut, but it also gives you an opportunity for delicious pickings you might otherwise miss—think new potatoes and young beans that can be added to salads in their pods.

Extending the Growing Season

If you have a greenhouse, this is already built into your game plan, but if you don't, there are still tricks you can employ to extend the life of your garden. Have a look in your garden center for cold frames, cloches, and fleece, and use this equipment to cover your plants in the winter and early spring. If you're growing in containers, you can also use bubble wrap or cardboard.

If you are using a greenhouse, be sure to add insulation against the frost if you want to keep growing through the winter.

❖ **Fun Fact:** Plants respond to sound. You might have laughed off stories about talking to houseplants to help them grow, but there's some truth in the tale: sound vibrations have been shown to affect plant growth.

5

THE EASIEST VEG TO START WITH FOR ORGANIC GARDENING

You have your tools, your soil is ready, your compost is coming along nicely, and you're ready to plan your vegetable garden. As we discussed in Chapter 4, my only real advice here is to plan for the whole year.

The rest is entirely up to you, and what you choose to grow will depend on your personal tastes and your growing region (see Chapter 11 for details). Be guided by these factors more than any other. As long as you're following organic principles, you will have rich soil filled with life and nutrition to support your plants.

However, if you're completely new to organic gardening, there are a few vegetables that might be good to start with, and a little guidance never goes amiss when you're starting out. Your seed packets will tell you the precise growing information you need for every plant, but we'll take a closer look at some of the easiest and most popular vegetables to grow in a new organic garden.

MUSHROOMS

I'm starting with mushrooms because they're unlike anything else you're going to grow. When I was narrowing down the list of vegetables to include here, I almost omitted them completely because they're not going to grow in your carefully prepared soil like everything else, and the process is quite different. However, not only are they fun to grow, but they will ramp up the biodiversity in your garden, so they're a great addition to an organic landscape. Growing them outside will take longer than it would indoors, but it's worth it for this reason.

Start by buying organic mushroom spawn from your garden center or online retailer. You can grow your mushrooms in coffee grounds or sawdust, but personally I prefer the log method, so that's what we'll look at here. If you're following this method, you'll need to buy spawn in a plug form, which just means it will be in wooden dowels.

You then need to source a log from a hardwood tree. If you're lucky, you'll already have something appropriate from when you cleared your garden to prepare your growing area. You want your log to be between 3 and 5 feet long, and no narrower than 3 inches in width.

You now need to drill holes in your logs. The longer it is before you use your log, the greater the risk of rotting, so start this process as soon as possible. Be guided by the instructions that came with your spawn plugs, which will tell you the size of hole needed to fit each plug. Aiming to leave a 2-inch margin at the top and bottom of your log, drill your holes in a diamond pattern. You want a space of around 6 inches between the top of your diamond and the bottom, and around 1 inch between the sides. You can make as many diamonds as you have space for (or spawn plugs to fill).

Follow the directions on your spawn packet to insert the plugs into the holes, and seal them with warm beeswax (again, your packet will come with precise directions).

Your mushroom logs can then be stored vertically against a wall in an area that gets a good amount of both sun and shade.

This is a slow process. You'll want to check on them regularly, but don't expect to see any action for at least 8 months. It could be much longer than this, sometimes taking well over a year. As soon as you do see them appear, it's all systems go: you only have about a week before they go bad, so harvest them quickly. To do this, you can either cut each mushroom from the base of the stem (where it emerges from the log), or you can twist them off.

Once you've collected your first harvest, knock the log onto the ground in a horizontal position, which should encourage further growth.

RHUBARB

Contrary to popular opinion, rhubarb isn't a fruit, it's a perennial vegetable. It's also pretty hardy and resilient, so it's a great one for beginners to start with.

Growing Conditions

Rhubarb is happiest in cooler climates, so it may not be the best for you if you're blessed with a lot of heat. It will need to be in full or partial sun with quick-draining soil, but if you're tempted to try it in a warmer region, aim for a spot with light shade. If you're lucky, rhubarb will thrive for over 5 years, so plant it somewhere that you won't need to disturb it. You will, however, need to mulch it well in the fall to keep it coming back strong.

Rhubarb's favorite soil pH is acidic—between 5.5 and 6.5, ideally. If your soil testing kit indicates that you need to increase the acidity, I've had some success with what I like to call "compost tea" (I don't think I invented the term, but I don't remember where I picked it up). Just leave a full watering can in the sun for 24 hours before adding compost to it. Stir it regularly for 48 hours, strain it, and then pour it over the area you want to plant. You could always use an organic fertilizer, of course. Once your rhubarb's in place, you can give it another dose of compost tea to keep it going.

Planting

You want to plant rhubarb in the later months of winter, or early spring. You could start it from seed, but it will take a while to get going, so I'd suggest planting a crown from an organic supplier. Set each crown about 4 feet apart to give it plenty of room to grow, and if you're planning more than one row, make sure they're about 6 feet apart. You may not need to do this though: you really don't need very much unless you're planning on feeding your whole community. Add compost and mulch to keep the area moist and prevent weeds.

Harvesting

Rhubarb might be easy, but it requires patience, and it should be left for two seasons to mature. When the time finally comes to harvest, hold the stem near the leaf and pull it away sideways. Try to avoid using a knife for this (the stub left behind will decay and encourage disease), and don't take all the leaves from one plant if you want it to keep coming back.

Storage

You'll be able to store whole stalks in your fridge for around 5 days, but they also freeze well: just cut them into chunks and stash them in freezer bags.

Potential Problems

One of the reasons rhubarb is good for beginners is that it doesn't attract many problems. However, there is a particular beetle (the rhubarb curculio) that can cause significant damage if it finds your plants. Your best bet is to pick it off when you find it and take it far away from your garden—or destroy it if you prefer.

Thinking About the Future

You can save rhubarb seeds, but in my experience, it isn't worth it. If you want more plants, you'd be best off taking a cutting from a thriving plant you already have.

TOMATOES

OK, so they're technically a fruit, but I don't know a single vegetable gardener who doesn't love a tomato, so they made the cut. I also know very few people who bother with store-bought tomatoes once they've started growing their own, so even though they're not as easy as some crops, I'd still recommend them to beginners.

Choosing Tomatoes

There are a huge variety of tomatoes to choose from. I wouldn't suggest starting with more than three types, but you can change up your varieties each year until you find your favorites. Tomato jargon can be a bit of a minefield for beginners though. You'll probably come across "determinate" tomatoes, "indeterminate" tomatoes, "heirloom" tomatoes, and "hybrid" tomatoes.

Determinate tomatoes fruit all in one go, and then they're over. They don't usually need much pruning, and you can often avoid staking them, but they do usually prefer hot, dry conditions.

Indeterminate tomatoes will fruit all summer, and their flowers appear all along the vine (rather than just at the end). You'll need to prune these regularly, and they nearly always need staking. These are your best option if you live in a humid area.

Heirloom tomatoes are "pure" varieties, bred for distinct characteristics. They're usually indeterminate, so you'll need to stake them and prune them frequently.

Hybrid tomatoes are bred through cross-pollination and don't self-propagate, so if you choose this variety, you'll only get one plant.

Growing Conditions

Tomatoes need sun, and lots of it. They need full sun for at least 8 hours each day, and if you don't have a space where you can give them this, you'll need to help them out a bit. You can do this by laying black plastic around them to soak up the heat (with the added bonus of pest and weed control). You could also hang a white sheet behind them to reflect the sunlight back to them, or you could cover them with row covers to emulate a greenhouse. Overheating is less likely to be a problem, but if you live somewhere very hot, you may need to cool your tomatoes down: if you notice stunted growth or dropped flowers, try shading them.

To conserve moisture in the soil, mulch around the base of your plants (this will also reduce the risk of disease). Beyond this, however, you don't need to worry too much about the soil, as long as it drains well. Tomatoes like a pH of between 5.8 and 7, which you should be able to achieve easily with compost.

Once your plants are safely in the growing area, they'll need deep and frequent watering, but be careful to avoid the leaves to reduce the risk of disease.

Planting

Your seed packets (or growing instructions if you buy seedlings) are the best place to look for planting details, as the exact requirements of a tomato plant depend on the variety. Whatever you choose, start them indoors a couple of months before the last frost date if you're growing from seed (which you'll have to if you're growing heirloom varieties). If you're buying seedlings, look for enthusiastic plants with lots of leaves, and don't choose plants that are flowering (you'll likely get a lower yield).

When you're planting outdoors, pay attention to spacing requirements: allowing your plants the right amount of space will ensure that they get the light and air they need to promote healthy growth and prevent disease. In general, staked tomatoes will need to be at least 1.5 feet apart, while unstaked varieties will need much more space —around 6 feet between each plant. You'll need at least 3 feet between each row too.

Once your plants reach about 1 foot tall most varieties will need training. At this stage, tie them to stakes that are at least 5 feet high. As they grow, remove smaller shoots and secure the stem to the stake, guiding it upwards.

If you're growing indeterminate varieties, you'll need to prune your plants as they grow suckers. If you don't, they'll eventually produce roots, flowers, and leaves which will reduce the size of the fruit.

Seed to Seedling

Sow your seeds in your starter mix at a depth of ¼ to ½ inch. Keep them moist, but don't soak them, and they should sprout within 2 weeks. A good way to keep them evenly moist is to cover your seed trays with cling film and keep an eye on them—don't let them get too wet, or mold will develop. As soon as you notice seedlings, take the cling film off the tray. Make sure they get at least 12 hours of direct sunlight a day, and as soon as you notice four leaves, it's time to get them into a bigger pot. When you do this, be careful not to damage either the stem or the roots. Transfer each plant into a new pot that's already been prepared with a layer of potting mix, and then fill with soil until only the leaves are left above the soil. You may need to do this once more if the plants reach a height of around 8 inches before it's time to take them outdoors.

You can do this once the soil temperature hits 55–60°F (13–16°C). Spend a week taking the containers outside to a shaded area for a couple of hours a day so they can acclimatize (this is known as "hardening off"). Then, ideally on a cloudy day, water your plants, pinch off the lower leaves, and prepare your growing area with compost, making a shallow hole for each plant. Gently remove the seedlings from their containers, transfer them to the growing area, top the holes up with soil, and water well. This process is known as "transplanting."

Harvesting

To get the best flavor, leave your tomatoes on the vine until you want to use them unless the temperature drops suddenly. They ripen best when the temperature stays around 75°F

(24°C). If you have to bring them in early, you can ripen them by putting them in a brown paper bag.

Potential Problems

Although they're easy to grow, tomatoes, unfortunately, are prone to both diseases and pests. If you're following the organic principles we outlined earlier, you'll have built up a healthy defense system, but you'll need to remain vigilant. We'll take a closer look at dealing with pests and disease in Chapters 7 and 8.

Thinking About the Future

You can extend your growing season by using your greenhouse or row covers in the spring. In the fall, you can prune away a lot of the leaves to make it easier for the sun to reach the fruit. When you're doing this, take off the flowers that remain to make sure the plant puts all its energy into the fruit that's already there rather than trying to grow more. If you're expecting frost, cover your plants with fleece, which should extend their life for a couple of weeks.

GARLIC

If you found tomatoes intimidating, garlic will be a welcome relief. It's almost too easy! It takes up very little space, and it's such a staple in so many kitchens that growing it is a must for most gardeners.

Growing Conditions

Garlic thrives pretty much everywhere as long as it isn't extremely dry. It needs full sun and nutrient-rich, quick-draining soil. As long as you dig plenty of compost into your growing area in the early spring, you can't go far wrong. You'll need to water it regularly for best results.

Planting

The ideal time to plant garlic is during the fall. Simply separate the bulbs into individual cloves and plant them with the pointy ends facing upwards and the root ends facing down. Bigger cloves produce bigger bulbs, so choose wisely! You want to plant them about 1 inch deep, with a space of about 1 foot between each row. Cover the soil with a good few inches of mulch to keep moisture in and weeds out. You can't really go overboard on mulch—up to 6 inches of it is fine. This will protect your garlic over the winter.

Harvesting

Your garlic should be ready for harvest in June or July. You'll know it's ready when its leafy tops start falling over. Use your fork to dig the bulbs out, and then tie them in bundles and hang them somewhere dry to cure for around a month.

Storage

Once your bulbs have dried, take the roots and tops off, and store them somewhere cool and dry. Most varieties will keep for 6–8 months, but check your packaging for details.

Potential Problems

Particularly with healthy soil, you're unlikely to run into problems with garlic, but there's a slight risk of finding onion maggot larva in the cloves. You'll be able to spot this by the dying leaves, but in the unfortunate event that this happens to you, there's little you can do. Just remove the affected bulb to prevent them from spreading.

Thinking About the Future

One of the best things about growing your own garlic is that you only have to buy it once. Once you've had a successful harvest, you can plant your new cloves for fresh bulbs next year. Your cloves will still be good for planting 6–8 months after harvest.

RADISHES

Everyone I met on my London allotment who had kids grew radishes. They're the most child-friendly vegetable to grow because you see results so quickly—often within 3 weeks. There are two kinds of radish: the quick-growing summer salad kind, and the winter variety, which take a little longer to reach maturity.

Growing Conditions

Radishes grow best during the spring and fall and need at least 6 hours of full or partial sun. They need watering frequently, and they will do well in nutrient-dense soil that drains quickly. Make sure your planting area is prepared well with compost, and dig it over to about 8 inches. If you're concerned about drainage, you can add sand to improve it.

Planting

You can sow your radish seeds directly into the planting area at a depth of about ½ inch. Remember your plan for continual harvest, and plant some every week in order to spread your harvest out. Rows should be between 8 and 18 inches apart, and you can plant around eight seeds for every foot. Continue to mulch with compost after planting, and don't let the soil dry out.

Harvesting

Your radishes will let you know when they're ready for harvesting: look out for bulbs poking through the soil. They're delicious when they're young, but pay close attention because they can quickly become spongy if they're left in the ground too long. If you opt for spring varieties, they will reach full maturity in 3–5 weeks. If you plant a winter variety, they'll take longer—about 2 months. Oddly enough, the time of day you harvest them makes a difference to their flavor—you want to pick them in the morning if you can.

Storage

You can't beat the flavor of a freshly picked radish, but they will keep in the fridge for up to 2 weeks if you remove the greens.

Potential Problems

The advantage of radishes is that the biggest threat is to their leaves, and since you don't eat that part, it's not so much of an issue. If you notice holes in the bulbs themselves, however, you may have root maggots. If you suspect that this may be the case, apply compost around the stem. For unaffected plants, spread a layer of diatomaceous earth or wood ash around the stems to discourage flies from laying more eggs.

Thinking About the Future

You can save the seed stalks of your radishes for next year's crop. Don't use the early bolting plants, but you can use others; when the pods are dry, separate the seeds from the stalk and save them for next year's planting.

PUMPKINS

Botanically speaking, pumpkins are another fruit, but most people seem to think of them as vegetables. It always surprises me a bit that something so big is so easy to grow. I find them particularly satisfying, just because the result is so significant that it feels like an achievement. If you're short on space, they're probably not for you, but otherwise, they're a great crop for beginners.

Growing Conditions

Space is the biggest requirement of the pumpkin, but it also needs full sun and plenty of water. Pick an area that's sheltered from the wind, and dig in a good amount of compost before planting. Dig over a large area, and till the soil well.

Planting

You can start your pumpkins from seed indoors, but be sure to harden them off before transplanting (it's the same deal as with tomatoes), and don't transplant them until the soil is consistently warm. You want to make sure the root system is always moist, but be careful when watering as wet leaves encourage fungus. As the weather gets warmer, mulch the growing area with compost to keep moisture in and discourage weeds.

You'll need to have one little extra trick up your sleeve with pumpkins unless you have regular visits from bees: you'll need to hand-pollinate them. Luckily this is a lot less complicated than it sounds: once you start to see flowers, simply pick a male flower and brush it lightly against a female flower. The male flowers have a slim stem, while the female ones have a bulbous growth on the main stem. If you've been encouraging biodiversity in your garden, however, there's a good chance that the bees and butterflies will do this for you.

Harvesting

It's not particularly difficult to tell when pumpkins are ready for harvesting: you're looking for a rich, solid color, a hard rind, and browning vines. They reach maturity within about 4 months. Just cut them from the vine, leaving about 2 inches by the stem, and wipe away the soil.

Storage

Pumpkins will keep well in a well-ventilated area that's cool and dry. To extend their shelf-life, put them on wooden shelves or pieces of cardboard, and keep them away from concrete flooring. Chunks of pumpkin will also freeze well, but you'll want to blanch them first.

Potential Problems

In a conventional garden, pumpkins are prone to pests, but your organic environment should limit your risk. Pests to watch out for include squash bugs, squash vine borers, and cucumber beetles. If you notice cucumber beetles, you run the risk of disease too: these little monsters spread bacterial wilt. Be wary of downy mildew and powdery mildew too, but if you have good air circulation in your planting area and give your plants plenty of space, you'll hopefully avoid this.

Thinking About the Future

You can harvest the seed from pumpkins that are 3 weeks past maturity. Just take them out, wash them, allow them to dry, and you'll have a good stash of seeds for next year's crop.

CARROTS

They're not quite as quick as radishes, but carrots are another vegetable to grow if you want to see results relatively quickly—they'll be ready about 70 days after planting.

Growing Conditions

Carrots like to be in full sun, but they can cope with a little light shade if necessary. Prepare the growing area with plenty of compost and remove any debris littering the soil. If your soil

contains a lot of stones that can't be removed easily, avoid planting long varieties. Check the balance of your soil before you plant too—if there's too much nitrogen in there, you'll get more foliage than root. The leaves are good in a salad, so they won't go to waste, but they're probably not what you're aiming for.

Planting

You want to sow carrot seeds directly into the growing area about 2 weeks before the last frost if you're planting in the spring, but you can also plant them during the fall (aim for about 10 weeks before the first frost). You'll need around 1 foot between your rows. Once they begin to grow, look out for about 2 inches of height in the tops. At this point, you will need to thin them so that there's no less than an inch between them. If they still look crowded after this, thin them again.

If you spot crowns coming up through the soil, add mulch to stop them from becoming green.

I usually add some compost tea a few times until the tops are about 5 inches tall.

Harvesting

From seed to maturity, you're looking at at least 50 days, but it could be up to 85. You can start harvesting your carrots when they're about the size of your finger. To make this easy, water them before you pull them up. That's an old trick of my dad's: he used to like to say he was taking them out for a drink before he evicted them.

Storage

You can keep fresh carrots in the fridge for a few days, but you can extend their life significantly by cutting off most of the stem and placing them in water before refrigerating. To store them over the winter, pack them gently in damp sawdust, and store them somewhere cool.

Potential Problems

Crop rotation is your key to avoiding pests and disease with carrots. Don't plant them where you've grown either carrots or parsley the previous season. You probably can't guard against slugs and snails though, especially when your carrots are still seedlings. Stay vigilant, and remove them when you see them. There's also some risk of the carrot rust fly. The best prevention for these critters (and indeed any flying pest) is to use a row cover.

Thinking About the Future

If you stored your carrots for the winter, you can use the tops for replanting next season. Just replant the whole carrot in the spring, and harvest the seed heads when they've dried out. Simply keep an eye out for the flowers, and cut them off when they begin to dry. Cut off the heads, and keep them in a paper bag until they dry out completely.

SWEET POTATOES

UK gardeners may have to put a bit more effort in with sweet potatoes: they're native to

South and Central America, and they prefer warmer conditions, but if you grow in polytunnels or greenhouses, you'll be fine. They can work outdoors too, but you might have to keep the soil warm with a black plastic sheet. Wherever you live, they're another one that needs plenty of space, so don't attempt them unless you can give them at least 15 feet for the vines to sprawl.

Growing Conditions

Sweet potatoes favor a slightly acidic pH (5.5–6.5), and ideally, a relatively sandy soil. The main requirement, however, is that the soil is warm and the last frost date has well and truly passed before planting. They will need quick-draining soil and full sun, and the soil should be well-balanced.

Planting

You want the soil to have reached 70°F (21°C) before you consider planting sweet potatoes, which will most likely be in the late spring. If you live in a colder region, or if you just want a head start, warm the soil up by using a plastic covering.

You'll be planting "slips," which are root-bearing stems. Soak them in some compost tea for a few minutes before you plant them (this reduces the risk of disease), and plant about 1 foot apart in rows with 3 feet between them.

Harvesting

It will be anywhere from 70 to 140 days before your sweet potatoes are ready for harvest. You'll know they're ready when their leaves begin to turn yellow, but make sure you dig them up before the first frost. Use your fork to loosen the soil, and then gently lift them out. Interestingly, unlike radishes, you don't want to eat them fresh out of the ground. If they're damaged, you'll need to use them quickly, but if you can avoid it, leave them to cure under a piece of cloth for around 10 days to develop their flavor.

Storage

Once they've been cured, store your sweet potatoes somewhere cool and dry, and check them after a couple of months for any damage. If you wrap them in newspaper you can extend their shelf life considerably.

Potential Problems

The most likely diseases to affect sweet potatoes are funguses. If you think your plants seem stunted, their leaves are drooping, or you notice black spots on them after harvest, you may have black rot. Unfortunately, there's not a lot you can do about this other than remove the tubers to prevent the problem from spreading to other plants. Your best bet is to rely on crop rotation and planting certified crops.

As far as pests go, rodents can be a problem in some climates. Conveniently, most of them seem not to like strong herbal smells, so try planting a good mint crop to discourage them. You may also run into problems with the sweet potato stem borer: key signs are holes on the stem and wilting leaves. A row cover is your best protection against these critters.

Thinking About the Future

If you want to have a go at growing from your own slips next year, save smaller tubers to sprout for next season. Tubers about 2 inches in diameter are ideal, but discard any with black spots.

PEPPERS

Again, if you're growing in the UK, you'd be better off in a greenhouse with peppers, as you'll get a better crop. They like a long season and plenty of sun, and as you know all too well if you live in the UK, that's certainly not guaranteed. For American gardeners, however, peppers are the second most popular vegetable to grow, and since they're not difficult, I'd be remiss not to include them.

Growing Conditions

Peppers need quick-draining soil and full sun, and they're most likely to set fruit when temperatures remain warm. The soil must be evenly moist, but not too wet, and the growing area should be prepared with compost before planting. You'll need to water them regularly, but carefully, being cautious to avoid wetting the foliage.

Planting

Start your seeds inside about 8 weeks before the last frost date, unless you live in a very warm climate, in which case you can sow them directly into the growing area once the soil temperature is over 55°F (13°C) at night. Once you're ready to transplant them, they will need to be in rows approximately 1.5 feet apart. If you're planting a tall variety (which your seed packet will tell you), you may also need to stake them.

Harvesting

The key to a strong crop is to harvest frequently: the more you harvest, the more you'll get. The majority of varieties are good to eat when they're still green, but the flavor will develop as they mature. You can expect your first harvest within 80 days of transplanting. Cut the peppers from the stem—don't be tempted to pull them off.

Storage

Fresh peppers will keep in an open plastic bag in the fridge for up to 2 weeks, or you can slice them up and freeze them.

Potential Problems

You'll most likely need your row covers for peppers as they're prone to insect damage. Particular nasties to watch out for are aphids, flea beetles, and cutworms. There are a few diseases they're susceptible to as well, including bacterial spot, blossom end rot, and anthracnose. Again, we'll look at problem prevention more closely in Chapters 7 and 8.

Thinking About the Future

To save seeds for your next planting season, choose peppers that are ripe with a rich color, and avoid any that show signs of disease. Simply take the seeds from the core and dry them out on a paper towel.

FENNEL

Fennel is a love-it-or-hate-it kind of deal. Personally, I love it, and it's enormously versatile: you can eat the leaves, the seeds, and the bulb, and all of them bring something different to the table. Go for a Florence variety if you want all of these benefits.

Growing Conditions

One of fennel's biggest selling points is that it's adaptable to different regions: in warmer regions, it will grow well as a perennial, but in cooler ones, it does fine as an annual. It will need a quick-draining area with plenty of sun. Soil-wise, it's not a big fan of clay, but otherwise, as long as the soil is slightly acidic (the pH can be as low as 5.5), it should be happy. Prepare the growing area well with compost before you plant.

Planting

Once the last frost date has been and gone, fennel can be planted straight into the garden. If you're in a warmer region and growing it as a perennial, think carefully about where to put it (it has a long taproot, so transplanting it won't be easy). Fennel grows surprisingly high, which means you'll need to think about the shade it will cast over the garden. It's also wise to keep it away from herbs, particularly dill, as they sometimes cross-pollinate, to neither of their benefits.

The soil will need to remain moist until you first notice leaves appearing, but after that, reduce your watering to a weekly schedule. Once you start to see the bulb swelling out of the ground, pile soil up around it to prevent it from turning green.

Harvesting

You can start harvesting the leaves while the bulb's still growing, but try to leave the flowers behind: they're great for encouraging biodiversity, as the pollinators love them. To harvest the bulbs, cut them at soil level.

Storage

You can keep fennel bulbs in the fridge for a week, and even longer than that if you remove the leaves. Unfortunately, fennel neither freezes nor dries well, so eat it as soon as you can after harvesting.

Potential Problems

One of the many reasons I love fennel is that pests don't, and it isn't prone to disease either. In fact, fennel does more good than harm in a vegetable garden, given the number of butterflies it tends to attract.

Thinking About the Future

While you want to leave some flowers to attract the butterflies, you can also remove a few heads to collect seeds for next season. Put the whole flower head in a brown paper bag and let it dry out—the seeds will naturally fall away.

ZUCCHINI (COURGETTES)

I think most people are familiar with the terminology now, but when I first moved to the UK, "courgettes" had me really confused. Zucchini and courgettes are one and the same, and you'll hear of them called "summer squash" at times too. They're another "vegetable" that's technically a fruit, and they have roaming vines, so you'll be best off growing them in a larger space.

Growing Conditions

All varieties of squash like full sun unless it's a particularly hot climate, in which case, partial shade is beneficial. They need rich, fertile soil and plenty of water. Till compost into the planting area before sowing your seeds, and in cooler climates, use black plastic to warm the soil.

Planting

You can plant zucchini directly into your growing area unless you're in a cold climate. In this case, you'll need to start your seeds inside about 4 weeks before you intend to plant them. When you're ready to plant outside, your rows will need to be about 2 inches deep and about 4 feet apart. Once your plants reach about 3 inches in height, you'll need to thin them out a bit. It's particularly important to avoid wetting the leaves, as it's prone to fungal disease. Your best chance of avoiding this is to water first thing in the morning. Personally, I find morning watering to be an almost meditative experience, so if you're anything like me, this will be no hardship.

Harvesting

The odd thing about zucchini is that it will keep growing if you let it, and if you're not careful, you'll end up with a monster too big for the fridge. To avoid this, harvest the fruit when it's about 6 inches long and 2 inches in diameter—probably after about 45 days. Cut them from the vine, along with about 3 inches of stem. You can eat the flowers too.

Storage

Zucchini will keep well in the fridge for a good couple of weeks, but you can also freeze it in chunks if you blanch it first.

Potential Problems

Zucchini is susceptible to fungus, so aim to keep the foliage dry. In terms of pests, it's the same as pumpkins: watch out for cucumber beetles, squash vine borers, and squash bugs—make use of those row covers! Crop rotation should keep any problems from

returning next season.

Thinking About the Future

You can save seeds for next season's planting by removing seeds from a harvest that is 3 weeks past maturity. Simply wash the seeds and allow them to dry.

❖ **Fun Fact:** There are over 100 species of carrot, and the original varieties were purple or white. The orange carrot we're all familiar with was actually bred from a yellow mutation.

6

AND SO IT BEGINS: PLANTING AND WATERING YOUR FIRST CROPS

We've explored some of the easiest vegetables to get started with, but your options are limitless, and you can choose to plant anything you like, depending on what you want to eat and where you live. Although we mostly discussed sowing seeds, if you're a true beginner, you may prefer to buy transplants from your garden center. That's often the easier option for beginners but bear in mind that if you do that, you'll want to check that they've been started organically. This is where you have the upper hand if you grow from seed: you can be more confident that they're truly organic—plus, the chances are, you'll have a wider variety to choose from.

What we'll do now is take a closer look at sourcing seeds, bulbs, and young plants, and get into the finer details of seed-sowing, before delving into the care you need to give your plants once they're in the ground.

SOURCING SEEDS, BULBS, AND YOUNG PLANTS

Your first year will always be the most challenging, but as soon as you've collected your first harvest you can begin collecting and storing your own seeds for next season. You can also take cuttings of successful plants. However, unless you do this, and certainly when you're starting out, you'll need to buy tubers, seeds, bulbs, and seedlings from your garden center. For an organic garden, you need to be mindful of the garden center's policies: some will stock plants that have neonicotinoids in the soil as a pest-prevention measure, and some will use peat and other pesticides. You may have decided that you're OK with using peat from sustainable sources, but whatever your stance is, you'll need to check with the garden center that it offers what you're looking for. All potting compost and soil should be certified organic, and pesticides should not have been used at any stage of the growing process.

If you know of other organic gardeners, another option would be to do seed swaps—or if you don't yet have seeds to swap, you could offer something else in return. I'd only really recommend this, however, if you know and trust the gardener, simply because you don't want to inadvertently bring in diseases or weeds.

One last word of caution: don't be tempted to take young plants from the wild. This will disrupt natural habitats and doesn't align with organic practices.

SOWING INDOORS VS. SOWING OUTDOORS

If you're reading straight through and you read about specific vegetables in Chapter 5, you'll already know the value of reading seed packets. This is where you'll find the recommendations for every vegetable you grow and where you're best off sowing your seeds.

The primary reason to sow indoors is that you're able to plant your seeds earlier and therefore get a head start on the growing season. This is particularly important in cooler climates because the growing season is shorter, and crops that grow more slowly (like tomatoes, for instance) won't have the time they need to reach maturity if you start them outdoors. Conversely, in warmer climates, starting seeds indoors can mean you get an extra harvest, so no matter where you live, there are reasons indoor-sowing is a good idea.

However tempting it is though, not every vegetable can be started indoors—some don't transplant well, and will do better if they're started on location. Root vegetables, for example, don't do well if their roots are disturbed, so it would be unwise to try starting them inside. Anything with a long taproot like parsley or fennel will be happier planted straight outside too.

But, of course, it's not as simple as "some don't transplant well and some do." Plants with slower root development (like celery and cauliflower) should be started indoors, as should tender crops like tomatoes and peppers. Some vegetables, however, are both tender *and* resistant to transplanting, and these should be sown outdoors, but not until the last frost date has truly passed. Examples of this tricky category are cucumbers, pumpkins, and squash.

I've put together a chart to help you decide whether to sow your seeds indoors or outdoors, but it's by no means comprehensive, so remember: check your seed packets!

Crop	Sow Indoors	Sow Outdoors
Arugula (Rocket, UK)		✓
Beetroot		✓
Broccoli	✓	
Brussels Sprouts	✓	
Cabbages	✓	
Carrots		✓
Cauliflowers	✓	
Celery	✓	
Cucumbers		✓
Eggplant (Aubergines, UK)	✓	
Green Beans		✓
Kale		✓
Lettuce	✓	✓
Onions		✓
Parsnips		✓
Peas		✓
Peppers	✓	

Potatoes		✓
Pumpkins		✓
Radishes		✓
Rutabaga (Swede, UK)		✓
Spinach		✓
Summer Squash (all varieties)		✓
Winter Squash (all varieties)		✓
Sweetcorn		✓
Sweet Potatoes		✓
Tomatoes	✓	
Turnips		✓

Tips for Indoor Sowing

As we discussed in Chapter 2, planning your planting is always advisable, and when it comes to seed-sowing, you'll thank yourself for having done so. Most indoor sowing will take place before you're ready to plant anything outside, and if you haven't planned ahead, you run the risk of missing your opportunity. Make sure you think about the size of your plot when you're sowing your seeds though: you'll need to allow for correct spacing once you transplant your crops, so there's no sense in sowing too many seeds just because you have a lot of seed trays.

That said, it's also wise to prepare for losses: not all of your seeds will germinate, and some may not survive transplanting, so while you don't want to go overboard, it's worth planting a few extra.

When it comes to sowing your seeds, the main thing to watch out for is that your containers are clean. You can use designated seed trays, or you can use containers of your own (I've had some great success with egg cartons), but whatever you use, they must be clean and have good drainage. If you're using egg cartons or some other repurposed vessel, that will mean making holes before you add your starter mix. I'll include a little more detail about containers a bit further down in the chapter.

The biggest mistake I've ever made with sowing seeds indoors was not labeling my containers. I was convinced I'd remember what I'd put where, but you can never trust your memory—and transplanting the wrong seedlings can lead to total garden confusion... so don't skip those labels! Make a note of the variety you're planting too—you'll thank yourself when you're trying to hone your favorites list for next season.

Once you've planted your seeds, you'll need to make sure they're kept at the right temperature and getting the right amount of light. Most will need at least 6–8 hours of direct sunlight, so you'll need to rotate your seed trays to make sure they all get an even share. If you struggle to get the right amount of light indoors (or if you want to start your seeds in the winter), you may need to consider a grow light. I'm very lucky with the levels of sun my house gets, so I don't have to worry about this, but I know plenty of people whose success doubled when they bought a grow light. The majority of seeds sprout best at 65–75°F (18–24°C), so keep an eye on the temperature as well as the light.

Lastly, it bears saying one more time: check your seed packets for their precise requirements. Some seeds need to be chilled, soaked, or scratched before they can be planted, and you don't want to skip this step.

A Note on Seed Containers

To align with the principles of organic gardening, it's important to repurpose and reuse as much as you can, so don't feel like you need to buy designated seed trays (although, of course, you can). Yogurt pots and ice cream containers make perfectly adequate seed containers as long as you clean them thoroughly and make holes in the bottom for drainage. The bigger ones will also take a couple of seeds at first, although once the plants grow, you'll need to transplant them into separate containers. Egg cartons, as I mentioned, are also a personal favorite of mine.

The seed trays you buy from a garden center are great if you're short on space, as they tend to be uniform in size and can easily be moved about. In the first few days, you can even stack them, but to be honest, as they ultimately need to be separated in order to get enough light, I wouldn't really recommend this. If you use seed trays, bear in mind that larger seedlings will need to be transplanted into larger vessels (probably more than once).

You can also buy seed trays with individual compartments, often referred to as "plug trays." The advantage of these is that root disturbance is kept to a minimum, and unless seedlings are large, they can often be transplanted straight from the plug tray to the growing area.

They're best for plants that will be transplanted within a few weeks, so they're a good option for radishes or salad greens.

Both seed trays and plug trays can be heavy on plastic use. If you want to cut down on your plastic, look out for those made from biodegradable fiber—and when you're done with them, you can add them to your compost heap.

SOWING YOUR SEEDS

Of course, not every seed is the same and you'll need to read your seed packets carefully, but who doesn't like a quick fix? Here's a simple step-by-step guide to sowing your seeds indoors:

1. Add your seed-starter mix to your (clean)

containers, and push it down until it's firm before adding a looser layer on top.

2. Use your fingertips to make shallow wells, and then add your seeds at the depth indicated on the packet. Most seeds will need pressing in gently, and if you know you won't be planting every seed in the packet, pick the biggest seeds (they're the most likely to germinate). Bigger seeds like beans should be sown in isolation (probably at a greater depth), but many can be sown in clusters of up to five seeds.
3. Sprinkle a little more of your seed starter over the top of the seeds, and make sure they're completely buried. Water them gently and evenly, and be careful not to flood them. My mom used to like to use a turkey baster for this—eccentric, perhaps, but highly effective.
4. Label your seed trays with the name of the vegetable, the variety, and the date of sowing.
5. Cover each container with a loose covering of cling film to stop the soil from drying out. Prick a few holes in the top to ensure ample ventilation and avoid mold growth.
6. Check the moisture of your containers regularly by lifting them. You'll know to add water if they're very light. What I like to do if this happens is fill a tray with water and place the containers on the tray. The soil will soak up the water and become

evenly moist. Just make sure to remove them once there are clear signs of moisture.

7. Once you begin to see seedlings, remove the cling film and position your containers in a bright, sunny spot. If you chose to stack your seed trays, now's the time to separate them.

TRANSPLANTING AND HARDENING OFF

There are few things more satisfying than the sight of healthy seedlings ready to set out in the big wide world. To give them their best chance, you need to give them a bit of TLC at the next stage.

When your seedlings are ready to transplant (you will judge this based on the directions on your seed packets, the temperatures outside, and the size and condition of your plants), give them one final water in their seed trays, but be careful not to overdo it. You want the potting mixture to be moist but not soggy. Make sure ventilation is good to decrease the likelihood of disease setting in and prepare your plants for the fresh air. Cool-season vegetables like onions, peas, and lettuce will be going straight into the ground as soon as the soil temperature is consistently about 50°F (10°C). As soon as you're confident that the soil is warm enough, it's time to transplant your seedlings: the younger they are when they arrive in the growing area, the more quickly they'll establish.

Some plants, however, will not be able to go straight into the ground and will need to be hardened off, as we saw with tomatoes. This process will take at least a week, but don't be afraid to make it two. Moving them too quickly from a stable environment can make them weaker and less likely to survive the varying conditions outdoors.

Broadly speaking, you'll want to start hardening off young seedlings around a week before the last frost date. Begin by watering them less frequently, and about a week before you intend to transplant them, take them outside to a shaded, low-wind area for a few hours each day. Little by little, extend the window of time your plants are outdoors, until, by the end of the hardening off period, they're outside all day. During this time, the soil should remain moist.

If you're growing in a greenhouse or cold frame, or if it fits better with your schedule, you may find it easier to increase the ventilation each day instead of taking the seedlings outside.

Once you're confident that your plants have been given enough time to adjust, you can transplant them. Ideally, this should be done on a warm but cloudy day, and as early in the day as possible. This will give your plants some time to acclimatize to the soil before the midday sun hits.

The Transplanting Process: Step by Step

1. Check the moisture of the soil the day before you intend to transplant: it should be moist but not soaked through. If necessary, water it well to make sure it's in the best condition for your young plants.
2. Rake over the soil to make it level and smooth.
3. Dig holes slightly wider than the root balls of the plants you're transplanting, approximately the same depth.
4. Carefully turn each container upside down, using your other hand to support the soil, and gently tap the bottom.
5. Transfer the seedling to the hole at around the same depth it was used to in its container, and add soil to cover the root ball.
6. Gently push down the soil to ensure the roots are in good contact with the soil.
7. Water the soil immediately to help the roots to settle.
8. A few days later, you can add an organic fertilizer or manure to encourage root development. You will also need to mulch at this stage if you live in a dry climate.
9. Keep an eye on the weather forecast so you don't get caught out by a surprise frost. If there's a cold spell due, protect your plants with a cloche overnight.

10. Continue to keep the soil moist, but do this by watering the soil directly rather than watering from above. You will probably need to do this about once a day, at least until your seedlings are established.

Sowing Seeds Outdoors

For seeds that are sown directly into the ground, you can obviously skip the hardening off and transplanting process. Your seed packets are, of course, the place to look to find out exactly when you'll need to sow them, but do bear your climate in mind too. Cross-reference your seed packets with the recommendations for your growing area (more on this in Chapter 11). As a general rule, however, most vegetables will need to be planted in the spring and summer, although you may well have a few left to plant in the fall.

To prepare the growing area for direct sowing, remove any weeds that have crept in since you prepared your bed, fork over the soil, and rake it to create a smooth and level surface.

Your seed packets will tell you whether you need to scatter the seeds or sow in drills, and also whether you need to do anything to your seeds before sowing.

Sowing in Drills: Step by Step

1. Use a trowel to create a shallow drill at the depth

specified by your seed packet. Generally, the smaller your seeds, the shallower the drill will need to be.

2. Water along the length of the drill.
3. Check the spacing requirements for your seeds on the packet.
4. For larger seeds, add them into the drills at the required spacing. For smaller seeds, tip a small amount into your palm, and then sprinkle them as thinly as possible along the drill.
5. Fill the drill with soil, and firm the area gently.
6. Add labels, specifying the crop, the variety, and the date of planting.
7. Water the row gently, taking care not to dislodge the soil.

Sowing Without Drills: Step by Step

Broadly speaking, your vegetables will require you to use drills, but some seeds, such as lettuces and radishes, can be scattered if you prefer. This is known as "broadcasting."

1. Mark the area you intend to sow using sticks or twine.
2. Prepare the soil by removing weeds, forking it over, and raking it to level out the top.
3. Scatter your seeds thinly across the whole area. I don't generally use the broadcasting method, but on the odd occasion that I do, I like to mix the

seeds in with a bit of sand to encourage a more even spread (the bonus is that it also makes it easier to see where you've scattered them).

4. Firm down the soil with a trowel.
5. Cover larger seeds with a light sprinkling of soil. You can get away without doing this for smaller seeds.
6. Water gently and evenly.
7. Add a label including details of the crop, variety, and date sown.

Sowing in Containers: Step by Step

If you're sowing in containers, the process is a combination of that used for sowing indoors and that used for sowing into the ground.

1. Prepare your containers by filling them with organic potting compost, and firm this down at a level just beneath the rim of the pot. You could use a starter mix for this as your young plants won't need the nutrients, but bear in mind that you will need to enrich the soil with compost later, or transplant the plants into a more nutrient-rich potting mix.
2. Press larger seeds directly into the compost (after checking the spacing requirements), and scatter small seeds thinly on the top.
3. Unless your seed packets tell you otherwise, cover

the seeds with a thin layer of compost.

4. Water gently, being careful not to dislodge the potting mix.
5. Label each container with the name and variety of the crop and the date of sowing.
6. Make sure the containers are positioned in a bright, sunny area, and be vigilant about watering (containers are more likely to dry out).

A Word on Watering

We've discussed watering quite a lot at each stage of the process, but I think it's helpful to boil it down here in order to make sure your garden stays in its best shape.

Bearing in mind water conservation (which we'll look at more closely in the next section) and the needs of your specific plants, aim to do the bulk of your watering in the morning. This will reduce the amount of water lost and decrease the risk of disease. Remember that you should aim to water the roots rather than the leaves. I like to do this by hand because it gives me greater control and allows me to waste less water, but you could use an energy-efficient irrigation system if you prefer. Once your plants are established, you will need to water less frequently. They'll generally only need about 1 inch of water each week, and if it's rained a lot, less of this burden will fall on you. Not only is this good for water conservation, but less frequent watering will encourage the roots to go deeper, ultimately producing stronger plants and a better harvest. Ideally, use water no colder than the temperature of the air—this is a good argument for using rainwater.

THE RESPONSIBLE USE OF RESOURCES

As you will recall from Chapter 1, one of the five building blocks of organic gardening is the responsible use of resources. It is at this stage of the process that you really need to think about this one: how you use water, energy, and materials reflects how well you're doing from an organic perspective. To keep you on track, we'll have a quick run-down of how to make sure you're using your resources as responsibly as possible.

Water

Obviously, you will need to water your plants regularly, but there are steps you can take to minimize your water use. Do your best to use as much rainwater as you can. I have a couple of rain barrels in my garden, which is an efficient way to collect rainwater without having to think about it. You can also use less water by adding compost and mulch to your soil to increase its capacity to hold water and reduce moisture loss. The less you have to dig, the better. Not only will this reduce water loss, but it will also cause less disruption to the soil. You can also be canny about when you transplant: just before the rain, for example, will require you to use less water than if you transplant at the beginning of a dry spell.

In a way, your garden will help you out with water conservation—in order to reduce the risk of disease, you're aiming not to water the foliage of your plants anyway. Watering this way will also decrease moisture loss through evaporation, and ultimately waste less. Similarly, you'll waste less water to evaporation by watering in the morning, and your plants will thank you for this too.

Energy

Domestic gardens aren't known for being super energy-heavy, but there are still a few things you can do to keep your energy consumption to a minimum. If you need lighting outdoors, for example, opt for devices that use solar energy. You could also use solar to power your greenhouse if you have one, or simply rely on manual vents rather than electronic ones. Growing seasonal crops will also mean you'll have less need for heat.

Wood

If you're building anything yourself, whether that's a compost bin, a garden shed, or a fence, you're likely to use wood. To align yourself closely with the best organic practices, try to source reclaimed wood, or ensure that it's local and sustainable. Be mindful of wood preservatives: very few are organic-friendly. You should be able to avoid using treated wood if you choose the right wood for the job—for example, hardwood for staking, which is more rot-resistant.

Plastic

Plastic is tough to avoid in the modern world, but many of us are waking up to the fact that we should avoid it where we can. Certainly, to be a true organic gardener you should aim to use any non-renewable resource as little as possible and have as little an environmental impact as you can. The reality is, however, that you'll almost certainly have to use some plastic, be that in the form of tools, a polytunnel, or a watering can. If you can, opt for recycled items, and try not to replace them unless absolutely necessary. Reuse plastic as much as you can (for example, by using yogurt pots for indoor sowing), and avoid using styrene.

MAINTAINING A HEALTHY GROWING AREA

This is also the time for us to revisit another essential building block of organic gardening: ensuring that the growing area remains healthy throughout the growing season. This means keeping both the soil and your plants in good condition and making sure that all your tools and containers are clean.

Plants and Soil

If you have been following the principles of organic gardening so far, you're already well on your way to maintaining a healthy growing area. Remember that the idea is to maintain a rich and active soil, which you'll be maintaining using your compost. All the plants you transfer to your growing area should be healthy and disease-free, and they should be well-suited to your soil and location. To encourage biodiversity and enable crop rotation, you should already have planted a mixture of different plants, providing a good habitat for wildlife and reducing the risk of diseases and pests. If you've followed the spacing directions on your seed packets, you will have set your plot up for good ventilation; maintain this by cutting back as necessary. Water wisely and carefully.

Tools and Containers

What may require a little extra thought is making sure all your equipment is clean. You will need to do this, not only to satisfy this building block of organic gardening, but also to reduce the risk of disease. That means washing down your greenhouse and any polytunnels you use as well as rinsing empty containers. Try to get into the habit of rinsing your tools after use too. This will reduce the risk of disease spreading from one plant to another, and minimize any temptation to use chemicals.

❖ **Fun Fact:** Did you know that gardening has been shown to reduce stress? It reduces our cortisol levels and encourages mindfulness, creativity, and mental focus. Plus, it's an easy way to get a good amount of physical activity into your life, which is also associated with lower stress levels.

7

ENEMY #1: DEALING WITH WEEDS THE ORGANIC WAY

The reason most people are hesitant to try organic gardening is the difficulty of dealing with weeds and pests without chemicals, but to me, one of the main delights about gardening this way is that the chance of *having* to deal with them is much smaller. It's true that you have to put a little more effort into creating a rich and diverse growing environment, but so long as you do this, you're likely to run into far fewer problems than you would with conventional gardening.

As we saw in Chapter 1, one of the essential building blocks of organic gardening is to avoid the use of harmful chemicals. Let's take a closer look at why this is important.

THE ARGUMENT AGAINST CHEMICAL WEEDKILLER

The reasons not to use chemicals in your garden can be boiled down to two main points: firstly, any chemical you use on weeds can also destroy other life—including the life in the soil you've worked so hard to enrich. This actually increases your chance of further problems with pests, weeds, and diseases later on. Secondly, chemical weedkillers contribute significantly to the pollution problem, both in the manufacturing process and through the chemical residue they leave behind.

The trick is to learn to live in harmony with the weeds. Dandelions, for example, don't deserve their poor reputation: they attract helpful pollinators and promote biodiversity in your garden. Nettles provide nutrients to your soil and compost and can be used to feed your plants. Any weeds that are actively invading your vegetable crops can be pulled up by hand—there's really no need to use chemical sprays.

MANAGING WEEDS THE ORGANIC WAY

Let's think for a moment about why weeds are a problem. The main reason is that they compete with your vegetables for valuable resources like nutrients, space, light, and water. They also have a habit of popping up as soon as there's an inch of free soil space. But they're not all bad: they encourage biodiversity and often attract useful pollinators to the garden. Think of them like your more difficult friends: you don't want them *not* to be at the party, you just need to manage them carefully.

That said, not every party needs to be full of difficult people, and certainly, when you're preparing your growing area, you'll need to clear away a lot of weeds. You'll do this through digging and mulching, as we discussed in Chapter 3.

Once your garden is up and running, however, your best defense against weeds is to stay on top of them. Obviously, you're tied to the spacing requirements of your crops, but where you have leeway, aim for close spacing to reduce the chance of a weed invasion. You can also cover bare ground with green manure or mulch. Beyond this, simply incorporate weed vigilance into your daily garden routine: every time you do your watering, add an extra 10 minutes to check for weeds and dig them out by hand.

CLEARING A LARGE AREA OF WEEDS

We covered how to prepare your growing area in Chapter 3, but if your land was particularly affected by weeds, you may need a little extra guidance. I'd still recommend dividing your plot in two and tackling only one half, mulching over one part of it while you deal with the other, but if you have very tall or dense weed coverage, you may need to cut them down first.

Begin by slashing down tall weeds. On one half, you're going to add your mulch. On the other, you're going to dig up weeds with deep roots (like dandelions). You can put the leaves in your compost, but drown the roots in some warm water for around a month before you think of composting them. This gives you a little extra bonus too: you can use the water to provide your plants with extra nutrients.

If you're unfortunate enough to be plagued by persistent weeds like ground elder or bindweed, you'll have to dig them over regularly, doing your best to take out as much of the root as possible. If you mulch over the offending area this job will be much easier. The bad news is that it can take a good couple of years of digging to get weeds like this under control, but the good news is that the whole process will enrich your soil.

When you're getting rid of persistent weeds like these, put the leaves and roots into a bin bag and let them decay into sludge before you compost them. Make sure the flowers and seed heads don't go into the bag though.

When you're putting in that much work, it can be tempting to clear everything, but if you can resist going for a full cull, leave a few weeds to grow. A small patch of nettles, for example, will be a beneficial addition to your vegetable garden: not only will it attract pollinators, but you can use the leaves to make a nutritious liquid feed for your plants.

HOEING YOUR VEGETABLE PATCH

There's a reason I included a hoe in your essential tools list: it's highly effective in the fight against weeds. You can use a hoe even when your vegetables are in place, guiding it between the rows to remove weeds without disrupting your crops. This is actually one of the reasons I prefer not to broadcast my seeds: having them in rows makes weeding much easier.

If weeds have already become a problem, you're too late and it's going to take much more work to remove them. Bear in mind that tiny weed seedlings are constantly developing beneath the surface of the soil—if you hoe regularly, you'll destroy them before they ever become an issue. Again, you can build this into your routine. It doesn't need to be a daily job, but perhaps you can make it a Sunday morning ritual to hoe between your vegetables. Prevention is always easier than cure.

Hoeing is best when the soil is dry on the surface (the weeds are less likely to reroot). It's another job best done in the morning too: any weed growth you uproot will dry out during the day.

To hoe efficiently and with minimal pain, try to stand upright. Make sure your blade is sharp enough to cut weeds from their roots, and push and pull it through the earth at a depth of about ½ inch.

❖ **Fun Fact:** If you were worried that not growing flowers might be a point against your garden attracting pollinators, take heart. Butterflies may be more attracted to weeds than they are to some flowers: they're more interested in the nectar than the color.

You might not love dandelions, but butterflies do.

8

ENEMY #2: DEALING WITH PESTS AND DISEASE THE ORGANIC WAY

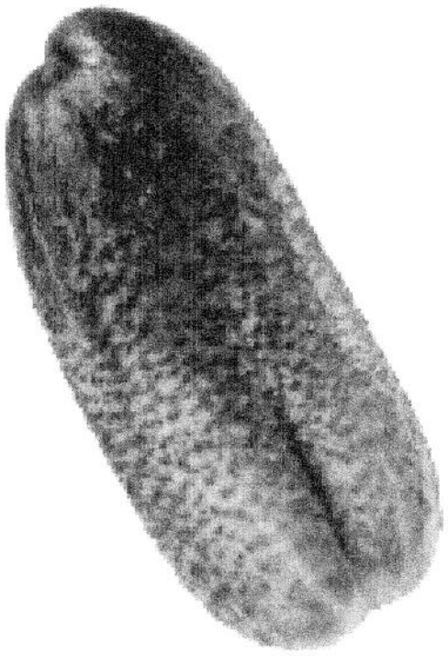

Still addressing the fourth building block of organic gardening, the avoidance of harmful chemicals, let's turn our focus to pests and disease. As with weeds, the good news is that nurturing an organic garden will naturally keep many issues at bay… but as with weeds, you can't escape problems completely. We'll begin by looking at the reason for avoiding chemical pesticides.

THE ARGUMENT AGAINST CHEMICAL PESTICIDES

The reasons not to use chemical pesticides are more or less the same as the reasons for not using chemical weed-killers: they're bad for other life forms and they contribute to pollution.

Just as with plant life, there are critters you actually want in your garden, and some of the chemicals used to kill insects will kill those too. Neonicotinoids, present in chemical pest sprays, will also affect helpful pollinators like bees, as well as non-harmful bugs that will help keep the pest population under control if they're left to their own devices.

Again, the trick is learning to live with the creatures in your garden. Aphids, for example, may be unwelcome visitors to your tomato plants, but they are a good food source for beneficial insects like ladybugs. Not many people have warm feelings toward slugs, but ground beetles and thrushes love them.

MANAGING PESTS AND DISEASE THE ORGANIC WAY

At the very heart of organic gardening is good health... and that means a garden that is free from problems caused by pests and disease. Just as we saw with weeds, prevention is your best line of defense, and that means being observant. Add to your daily weed check a check for diseases and insects, many of which will be prevented by your maintenance of a healthy growing area. A biodiverse garden is a resilient one, and at its best, all species will work in tandem to manage problems as they arise. Insects will pollinate your plants, worms will enrich the soil, and birds will eat disruptive insects like aphids. As soon as you bring chemicals into the equation, you disrupt this natural harmony, ultimately encouraging more problems.

Continue to encourage biodiversity in your garden and keep a careful watch over your plants. Pick off pests as you spot them and remove any infected leaves. You can also remove pests with water when they're too small or too many to remove by hand. It pays to educate yourself a bit about the critters that inhabit your garden too: make an effort to learn which insects are harmless and which to watch out for. The more you learn about them, the better placed you will be to develop strategies to defend against them.

If you do notice a particular problem, use your crop covers and try to create barriers using organic ingredients like oats, wool, and grit to discourage slugs. In some instances, particularly in your garden's infancy, you may require a tougher strategy. If this is necessary, look for biological treatments like nematodes. You could also try pesticide-free sticky traps, but if you do this, make sure to raise them slightly above the ground so you don't end up subjecting helpful and harmless insects to collateral damage.

There's no way to cover every pest or disease you might encounter in every growing region, but let's take a look at some of the most common enemies of vegetable gardeners and how you can manage them organically.

COMMON PESTS AND STRATEGIES FOR DEALING WITH THEM

Pest	What Is It?	Symptoms	Prevention & Treatment
Allium leaf miner	Tiny white maggot commonly found on onions and leeks.	Leaf splits, distorted plants, and white spots.	Clear the plot after harvest and dig over the soil. Soak infected plants for 2 weeks before adding to compost. Cover crops with mesh to prevent flies from laying eggs.
Ants	Black and red ants are common in most gardens, usually laying eggs in the late summer.	Ants harvest the residue exuded by aphids and can therefore carry their diseases. Nests can disrupt the soil, causing plants to a habit of stealing freshly sown seeds.	Complete removal of ants is almost impossible, but you can water their nests with nematode treatments and encourage natural predators like frogs.
Aphids	Commonly found on a wide range of vegetable crops on roots, leaves, and stems. They are one of the most common pests and can sometimes carry diseases.	When they're found in large numbers on younger plants, they can cause shoots to weaken, sometimes resulting in the death of the plant.	Encourage predators like birds, bats, and insects. Growing flowers to attract ladybugs and hoverflies can help. Attract blue tits with fat balls. Inspect plants frequently, and remove aphids as soon as you spot them.
Pigeons	For vegetable gardeners, most birds won't cause a problem but watch out for pigeons if you're growing brassicas.	Pigeons will eat brassicas if they have easy access.	Try using netting to put a barrier between your crops and the pigeons.

Cabbage Whitefly	Small insect with white wings found underneath brassica leaves. When disturbed they fly upwards in clouds, leaving behind the young.	Whiteflies can cause stunted growth and plant distortion. Their young leave a sticky substance on the leaves.	The good news is that many plants can tolerate whiteflies. You can limit their damage by maintaining good soil health to encourage strong plants. Try planting cilantro (coriander, UK) and fennel to attract parasitic wasps to consume the young. Remove infected leaves before the young mature.
Carrot Fly	Shiny black flies with red heads, transparent wings, and orange legs. Their larvae are roughly the same size as the adults, and creamy white in color	Young seedlings may not survive, and established plants can become infested with brown holes or suffer foliage loss.	Aim to sow thinly to limit thinning. Weed around carrots and harvest them on a dry, windless evening or on a day with high winds (bruised leaves will attract them). Grow near onions, which will mask the smell of the foliage. If carrot flies are a problem, try covering your plants with fleece
Greenhouse Whitefly	Tiny moth-like insects with creamy yellow bodies and white wings.	Underside of leaves may turn yellow from their excretions and develop black mold.	Maintain a healthy soil to encourage resistant plants, and keep all tools and equipment clean. Discard infected plants.
Leek Moth	Tiny brown moth with patchy yellow-green caterpillars.	Caterpillars burrow into plants, eating the bulb and stem and leaving white and brown patches on the leaves.	Destroy any infected plant and dig over the area. Protect your plants with fleece coverings, and pick off caterpillars as you spot them. Encourage natural predators like bats, frogs, and birds.

Slugs and Snails	Soft-bodied mollusks that secrete slime. Slugs are active all year, but snails hibernate during the winter. Both feed mostly at night, but snails can climb higher to do so.	Slime trails are the first sign of slugs and snails. Seedlings are often completely eaten, and you may find large holes in the leaves of mature plants.	Use multiple methods to protect vulnerable crops, renewing barriers (like wool, oats, and grit) after the rain. Encourage natural predators like birds, frogs, and hedgehogs, and pick off slugs and snails when you spot them. Beer traps usually work on slugs, but raise them off the ground so as not to also kill beetles. Nematodes are also effective.
Wireworm	The larvae of a range of click beetles, these critters have golden bodies and three pairs of small legs (found behind the head)	Attacks roots, tubers, and stems, particularly of carrots, potatoes, and beetroot, leaving small holes. This can cause fungal and bacterial rots.	Digging exposes larvae to predators, and harvesting root vegetables early limits the damage they can cause.
Moles	Small velvety mammal with large claws. More common in organic than conventional gardens because of the rich supply of worms.	Leave molehills and may disrupt vegetables.	For persistent problems, an expert will be best placed to trap them humanely. If you have space, try planting Euphorbia to discourage them. They are also deterred by vibration, noise, and the scent of urine.
Pea and Bean Weevils	Small, short-snouted creatures, brownish-gray in color with white legless larvae. Found in the soil surrounding peas and beans.	Eats the leaves of pea and bean plants, leaving semi-circular holes. Can lead to loss of seedlings, and sometimes get into beans and pods.	Maintain good growing conditions to create strong resilient plants. Beyond this, there's little you can do to discourage them.

COMMON DISEASES AND STRATEGIES FOR DEALING WITH THEM

Disease	What Is It?	Symptoms	Prevention & Treatment
White Rot	A disease that affects allium roots.	Causes roots to rot, and sometimes leaves a fluffy white mold. Plants may die, with older leaves wilting and producing a sour smell.	Crop rotation is the best treatment, as the disease can survive in soil for up to 20 years. If you have a small infected area, consider isolation. Don't put infected plants into the compost, and ensure that all tools are clean before reusing.
Tomato Blight	A fungus affecting tomatoes.	Dark brown patches inside yellow rings on the leaves. As with potato blight, this will spread to the whole leaf. Leaves may also show a white coating underneath and stems may develop dark streaks. Fruit may acquire dark marks and white mold.	Aim to keep the leaves dry and encourage ventilation. Look for resistant breeds and early-fruiting varieties. Avoid composting affected fruit.

Downy Mildew	A gray/purple mold found on leaves, usually during cool, wet conditions.	Affects chives, onions, and shallots. Leaves develop mold and die.	Destroy all allium debris after the growing season and do not compost infected plants. Prioritize good drainage, ventilation, and spacing, and destroy any plants that sprout too early.
Leek Rust	A disease affecting leeks.	Leaves develop rust-colored pustules during the summer. Leaves may die and growth may be stunted.	Water plants well during hot, dry conditions. Limit nitrogen by using only well-rotted manure.
Chocolate Spot	A fungus affecting fava beans (broad beans, UK).	Stems, leaves, and pods develop brown spots and plants die early.	Encourage good ventilation and improve soil drainage. Remove infected plants and discard the seeds.
Botrytis	Gray mold found on bean pods.	Gray, wet lesions on pods.	Prioritize good drainage and ventilation. Remove petals stuck to pods and discard the seeds of infected plants.
Powdery Mildew	A disease affecting beetroot, spinach, and chard, as well as cucumbers and squash. May also be seen on peas.	A powdery gray coating on leaves, most common in hot, dry conditions. On cucumbers and squash this may be a powdery white coating seen at the end of the season, and is not usually a problem. It also appears powdery white on peas.	Prioritize moisture retention in the soil and aim to plant resistant varieties. Water only in dry weather and pick regularly to encourage new growth. If spotted on peas, treat with a homemade bicarbonate of soda solution.

Clubroot	A disease affecting brassicas.	Plants may wilt in dry conditions and then may look stunted with a purplish tint to the leaves. Roots swell, often producing galls.	This disease often arrives on plants, so select new crops carefully. It can survive for up to 20 years in the soil, so employ crop rotation, and try adding lime to the soil. Raise brassicas in pots before transplanting if you think they may be affected. Keep tools and equipment clean.
Cucumber Mosaic Virus	Disease affecting cucumbers and squash.	Young leaves may show signs of mottled yellowing and distortion and the growth is stunted. Often results in a poor harvest and pock-marked fruit.	Remove infected plants and choose resistant varieties.
Potato Blight	A common disease affecting potatoes.	Dark brown spots inside a yellow ring, quickly spreading throughout the leaf. Leaves rot quickly.	Cut the leaves from infected plants, and avoid harvesting for 3 weeks. If potatoes are seen at the surface of the soil, mulch with straw or leaves to stop them from turning green. Grow resistant varieties and avoid leaving infected potatoes to sprout on the compost heap.
Scab	A disease affecting potatoes.	Brown marks on potatoes (although they can still be eaten if peeled).	Plant resistant varieties and prioritize water retention in the soil. Avoid adding lime to the soil before planting potatoes.

❖ **Fun Fact:** Snails move at a pace of about 0.66 inches per minute. If they were to move without resting, they'd travel only one-tenth of a mile in a week. You shouldn't have any trouble catching and relocating them!

9

SUCCESS! HARVESTING AND STORING YOUR BOUNTY

Guess where you're going to find your harvesting instructions? Yep, it's on your seed packets! We've already looked at harvesting and storage techniques for all the vegetables we discussed in Chapter 5, but if you're new to organic gardening, you may need a little more guidance. We'll take a look at some general harvesting tips to cover a few other crops you may have planted. Of course, it's still not an exhaustive list, so consult those seed packets if you're growing something different or you need more detailed guidance.

ALLIUMS

Harvesting

When the leaves of onions and shallots are falling over they're telling you it's time to harvest.

Storage

Keep all alliums somewhere hot and dry for a few weeks. Once their skins are papery and dry, they can be stored. You can plait garlic into ropes and onions can be hung or stored in net sacks with good ventilation. Their ideal storage temperature is 36–39°F (2–4°C), and they must be kept from freezing.

ASPARAGUS

Harvesting

Growing asparagus is playing the long game: it will be 3 years after planting, when the spears are 6–9 inches tall, that you can harvest them. To do this, cut or snap each spear at ground level.

Storage

Keep the spears upright and store them in a cool, moist environment for up to 2 weeks.

Asparagus can be frozen after blanching.

BEETS

Harvesting

Beetroot is ready for harvesting when it is between 1¼ and 3 inches in diameter. Hold the base of the greens and pull the root out of the ground. You can brush away the soil but avoid scrubbing the root as this will damage its skin.

Storage

Beetroot should be stored without its head in a cool, moist environment, where it will keep for about 5 months.

BROCCOLI

Harvesting

You want to harvest broccoli while its buds are still green and closed. Simply use a sharp knife to cut the head away from the plant.

Storage

Broccoli will keep for about 2 weeks in a cool, moist environment. It can also be frozen after blanching.

CABBAGES

Harvesting

Harvest your cabbages once the heads are firm and before the first frost, cutting them from the stem at the lowest point you can. Aim to leave about 6 inches of stem attached to the head.

Storage

Store cabbages on slatted shelving lined with a thick layer of newspaper, where they should keep for about 5 months. The ideal temperature for this is 32–39°F (0–4°C).

CAULIFLOWERS

Harvesting

Your cauliflowers are ready to harvest when they're white and firm. Cut them from the stem, leaving a few outer leaves for protection.

Storage

They can be stored in a cool, moist environment for around 3 weeks, and can be frozen after blanching.

CUCUMBERS

Harvesting

Cucumbers can be harvested once they've reached about 6 inches in length. Cut the fruit from the vine, taking about 1 inch of stem with it.

Storage

Cucumbers should be stored in a cool environment, ideally the fridge, for around a week.

EGGPLANT/AUBERGINES

Harvesting

Eggplant should be harvested before its color dulls. Cut the fruit from the plant, taking 1 inch of stem with the fruit. Do this carefully as eggplant bruise easily.

Storage

Eggplant can be stored in a cool environment for around a week.

FRENCH AND RUNNER BEANS

Harvesting

Wait for the pods to reach a length of about 8 inches before harvesting and aim to pick them every few days to avoid them becoming stringy. The more you harvest, the more beans the plant will produce.

Storage

Gluts are common with these crops, but they freeze well. You could also allow some pods to set seed, shelling them when they're dry and storing them inside a paper bag.

LEEKS AND BRUSSELS SPROUTS

Harvesting

Although these crops are in different families, I've grouped them together because they can often be left in the ground throughout the winter. However, if you're expecting very bad weather, it may be wise to harvest them early. To do this, dig up the whole plant, roots and all, and place them in water.

Storage

Both plants will keep for around a week in a cool environment if harvested early, with Brussels sprouts lasting around a month otherwise.

LETTUCES

Harvesting

Most lettuce is ready for harvesting when the

leaves are 3–6 inches long, and you will be able to harvest continually until the plant begins producing flowers. Use your garden snips to cut the leaves off close to the stem.

Storage

Lettuce will keep for around a week in a cool, moist environment.

PEAS

Harvesting

The right time to harvest peas depends on whether or not you want to eat the pod. For eating, pods can be picked when they're flat, or you can wait until they're swollen if you intend to shell them. In either case, they can be picked directly from the plant.

Storage

Peas will keep for about a week in a cool, moist environment. They can also be frozen after blanching.

ROOT VEGETABLES

Harvesting

Bear in mind that potatoes have slightly different storage needs than other root vegetables, although the harvesting procedure is the same. Root vegetables should be dug up carefully, before removing their leaves by twisting them near the crown. For potatoes, aim to harvest them when it's dry and cool and leave them in the open air for a few hours before storage. Brush away the soil, but avoid scrubbing the roots as this can cause skin damage.

Storage

The majority of root crops can be stored in shallow boxes with slightly damp sawdust between each layer. They should be stored in a cool environment, ideally at 32–39°F (0–4°C). Potatoes, however, should be stored in a dry, dark place in paper sacks, ideally at a temperature of 41–50°F (5–10°C), where they should keep well for around 6 months.

SWEETCORN

Harvesting

Corn is ready for harvesting when the silks have turned brown and are dry to touch. If you press the end of your fingernail into the kernels, they should be creamy. Hold the ear firmly, and then pull it downwards, twisting and pulling the ear away from the stem.

Storage

Sweetcorn will last for around 5 days in a cool, moist environment. It will also freeze well when the kernels are removed from the ear and blanched.

❖ **Fun Fact:** The word "harvest" is derived from the Old English word for fall/autumn, haerfest, corresponding with the time of year that most crops are ready for harvesting.

10

THE YEAR AT A GLANCE: A MONTH-BY-MONTH GUIDE FOR YOUR VEGETABLE PLOT

Your month-by-month garden plan will need to be adapted according to the region you live in, which we'll look at more closely in Chapter 11. It's also highly dependent on the crops you want to grow. However, I personally find that it's good to work with a template when you're starting out with something new, so I've put together a rough guide to help you plan a whole year. Don't be tempted to skip planning out your year—

following a plan, however rough, will help you keep on top of your garden, and it will make maintenance much easier to manage. As you grow in experience, you may want to make changes and tailor your plan more closely to your garden. One of the things I love about gardening is that you grow with your garden, and every year you learn new ways to tweak your plan and make the next growing season even better.

I have based this plan on USDA Zone 5 (USA), which corresponds with Hardiness Zone H7 (UK). Bear in mind that it is only a very loose outline to help you create your own plan.

DECEMBER/JANUARY

Soil

You will need to cover the soil during the coldest months of the year. The fall leaves can be used as mulch and you can also use fleece (this is particularly useful during windy weather, when mulch may be disturbed). Tempting as it is to stay indoors, don't neglect your weeding duties. Continue to hoe and pull out weeds, and dig out any perennial weeds that have taken root. Remember that you can compost the leaves but don't include seed heads or perennial roots.

Fallen leaves can be continually collected and kept in bin bags to make leaf mold. However, throughout all your activity, be mindful of walking on wet soil. Do this as little as possible in order to preserve its structure and keep it in good health for the spring.

Composting

I tend to find that there's a greater quantity of wet waste from my kitchen caddy at this time of year. If this happens to you, balance it with dry waste like paper and cardboard. Keep turning your compost heap to aerate it.

If you're feeling ambitious, this is a good time of year to make a compost trench. Dig a furrow about the depth of your spade in the space where you plan to grow legumes, and fill it with the old stems of brassicas. You can also add other raw vegetable scraps. Once the trench is

full, cover it with soil. This will feed the soil over winter, creating a fertile area for next year's growth.

Vegetables

You won't be planting much during this time but there's still some work to be done. Garlic, after all, can be planted right through until March. You will also be able to do some indoor sowing for some early plants. Some varieties of carrot, spinach, and lettuce work well for this, and if you have a greenhouse, you'll have even more chance of early sowing.

Beyond this, winter is a good time to plan your crop rotation.

Pests and Disease

If your alliums suffered the wrath of allium leaf miners or leek moths, now is the time to dig over the plots. This will help bring pests to the surface and provide a welcome meal for the birds. Try hanging fat balls to encourage birds to visit. If you have winter brassicas, remove any yellow or dead leaves to reduce the risk of pests and further disease.

Maintaining a Healthy Growing Area

Most gardens will be full of spider nests at this time of year, and this is perfect for your garden. Don't be tempted to disturb any nests you find: spiders are great at pest control. If you live in the UK, watch out for caterpillars if you're harvesting holly and ivy for the festive season: these are probably going to turn into Holly Blue butterflies, and they depend on holly and ivy for survival.

Greenhouse (if You Have One)

This is a good time to clean your greenhouse. Dislodge any whitefly you come across and wash down any infected area. Remove any dead leaves from plants to reduce the risk of mold.

Soil

At this stage, bare soil should remain covered with mulch to protect the micro-organisms living in it and preserve its structure. Continue to stay off wet soil as much as possible. I like to make walkways using boards to reduce compaction. If you have clay soil, now is a good time to add grit to improve drainage.

Composting

Turn your compost heap to aerate it, and as you do this, keep an eye on its moisture level. If it looks too wet, add dry, carbon-rich materials like twigs and cardboard. If it looks too dry,

add more kitchen waste and some water. If you're making leaf mold, add water to the bags to boost decomposition.

Vegetables

If you haven't yet planned your crop rotation, do so now. You can also start digging in green manure if the soil is dry enough. If you plan to grow fava beans (broad beans, UK) or parsnips, you can sow them as soon as the soil reaches 41°F (5°C). Wait a little longer if the soil is very wet or you have clay soil.

Pests and Disease

Continue removing dead foliage to reduce the risk of disease. Watch out for early colonies of aphids if the weather warms up suddenly, and remove them as soon as you spot them.

Maintaining a Healthy Growing Area

Continue to hoe the land to bring insects to the surface for the birds. You can also dig a compost trench if you didn't do this in January.

Greenhouse (if You Have One)

With your greenhouse clean, you can turn your attention to your containers, ensuring they're clean and ready for planting. Scrub everything well in hot water with a mild organic detergent. If any algae has developed since you cleaned your greenhouse, clean this off and sweep away any other new pests.

MARCH

Soil

Promote good soil structure by continuing to avoid compacting wet soil. As the weather begins to get warmer, spread well-rotted manure and compost onto the soil. If you have planned to leave any area uncultivated until later in the year, you could consider sowing a green manure like fenugreek to enrich the soil.

Composting

Turn your compost heap again to promote air circulation, being careful not to disturb hibernating wildlife. If you have compost that's ready to use, empty it out of your compost bin, and store it in sacks ready to use as necessary.

Vegetables

It's a good idea to warm the soil with a plastic sheet or cloche at this time to prepare it for sowing. Crops that were planted in the fall should be surrounded by compost to encourage spring growth. Any of last year's potatoes that are still in the ground should be dug up too, and the stumps of brassicas should be removed and composted.

Pests and Disease

This is the time of year that aphid numbers creep up as their usual predators aren't yet around to control the population. Stay vigilant, and remove them when you see them.

As you prepare for sowing and transplanting, a few strategically placed slug traps are a good idea. Remember to raise them above ground level to avoid trapping other species.

Maintaining a Healthy Growing Area

You may be primarily growing vegetables, but for the sake of biodiversity, it's worth planting some flowers at this time of year if you have the space. The sooner you can attract helpful predators and pollinators to your garden, the better. For ultimate pest control, aim to attract beetles, ladybugs, and wasps.

Greenhouse (if You Have One)

This is your last chance for greenhouse and container cleaning if you haven't done this already.

APRIL

Soil

In many areas, April is a time for rain, so continue to be careful not to compact the soil.

Composting

I like to take the top layer off my compost around now and rake it through, before removing the compost that's ready to use. Then I add the top layer back into the compost bin to give it an extra boost.

Vegetables

It's likely that your soil will still be cold, so delay outdoor sowing until you see strong evidence of weeds. Keep on top of the weeds, and remove any vegetable plants that have self-seeded without you realizing. If you're unable to deal with high-weed areas immediately, cover them with black plastic to stop further growth.

Once the conditions are right, you will be able to plant some of your crops, so prepare the area with compost and manure. Protect crops sown outdoors with cloches and monitor your seedlings if you have started any indoors.

Pests and Disease

For indoor sowing, reduce the risk of fungus growth by sowing thinly and watering carefully. If you live in a warm climate, watch out for asparagus beetles near the end of the month, removing them as soon as you see them. You will have a lot of young plants at this time, so do everything you can to protect them from slugs. Allium leaf miners and leek moths lay their eggs in April too, so protect your seedlings with fleece.

Maintaining a Healthy Growing Area

Continue to hoe the land and remove weeds, and add compost to any areas still awaiting crops. Don't miss the opportunity to improve your soil if you have free space.

Greenhouse (if You Have One)

Your seeds and seedlings will need regular attention this month. Water them carefully and transplant them as soon as they're ready.

MAY

Soil

Continue to improve the structure of your soil with well-rotted manure and compost. If you have free space, consider planting something like crimson clover, which is a good green manure plant and grows quickly. This will both feed the soil and keep the weeds at bay.

Composting

You'll have noticed that you're using a lot more compost now, so keep building your pile, remembering to mix greens and browns for a healthy balance.

Vegetables

In most regions, the soil will be warming up now, so you should be able to plant some of your more delicate crops. Mulch around the tops with last year's compost and keep on top of your hoeing duties to minimize weeds. If you have a lot of space between crops, you could plant a quick-growing green manure around them to promote growth and soil fertility.

Pests and Disease

Slugs will be very active this month, so stay vigilant, and do what you can to deter and remove them. This is also the time for carrot flies, so use fleece barriers to protect your carrots. In fact, May is the time you're likely to see quite a few pests emerging. Use your row covers, pick off unwelcome visitors when you see them, and encourage natural predators.

Maintaining a Healthy Growing Area

Focus your efforts on encouraging biodiversity. The more helpful visitors you can attract, the better your chances of pollination, and the lesser your risk of pest infestations.

Greenhouse (if You Have One)

It should now be very warm in the greenhouse, which means biological controls for indoor pests will work. If necessary, you can use biological agents to control aphids and whiteflies in the greenhouse.

JUNE

Soil

If you have any unused soil, mulch it with compost to deter weed growth and lock in moisture.

Composting

Continue to add to your compost bin, turning the pile regularly to promote airflow. If you worry at any point that it looks dry, feed it with some water and turn it again.

Vegetables

You still have plenty of time for sowing, so if you had a disappointing start with some of your crops, you have a chance to sow again. The soil will be warmer now and you should have been improving it continuously, so this next batch may be more successful.

Pests and Disease

Remain vigilant against pests like aphids, but be careful not to destroy insects that aren't posing a threat to your crops. Wasps tend to be nesting at this time, but you needn't remove them unless they're in a really dangerous spot. Leave them alone and they'll do nothing more invasive than eat a few pests for you. Continue to use your crop covers and fleeces to protect against pests, and pull up any plants showing signs of disease. Water appropriately to reduce the risk of rot.

Greenhouse (if You Have One)

Use biological pest controls as necessary in the greenhouse and keep on top of ventilation.

Watch out for sun scorch on leaves (indicated by brown marks), adding shading if necessary.

JULY

Soil

Continue to mulch unused areas to reduce moisture loss and keep up a daily weeding regime.

Composting

I've never not had to water my compost at this time of year—as soon as it starts looking dry, you know you need to add water. Keep adding green and brown waste in equal measures, and turn the pile regularly to aerate it.

Vegetables

It's still too early to despair if any of your crops have failed: there's still plenty of time to sow. If you plan to take a summer vacation, prepare your garden by hoeing, weeding, and mulching.

Pests and Disease

If you need to thin your carrots, remember that the scent of the leaves will attract carrot flies, so use a barrier to protect them in the early days after thinning. Brassicas are under threat from cabbage white butterflies at this time of year, so protect them too. Protect root crops from disease by digging up any infected plants and mulching with leaf mold.

Greenhouse (if You Have One)

Ventilation is key at this time of year, so leave doors and windows open when you can. Water carefully and check your plants regularly for disease. You can continue to use biological pest controls if necessary.

AUGUST

Soil

Keep adding mulch and compost to keep the soil in its best shape. This is a great time for sowing green manure, particularly if you've had early harvests and are left with bare soil. Continue to hoe religiously.

Composting

Keep feeding your compost with an equal mix of green and brown waste. Water it as necessary and add nettles and lawn trimmings if you can to speed up decomposition.

Vegetables

It's all hands on deck in the garden at this time of year. Keep a constant watch over your vegetables, regularly harvesting those that need it. Your tomatoes will probably need tying, and you'll need to remember to pinch out their suckers. To help fruits like zucchini (courgettes) and pumpkins ripen, cut off their old leaves. Most of your alliums will need harvesting about now too.

Pests and Disease

This is the prime time of year for tomato and potato blight, so keep an eye out for these conditions (see Chapter 8). Watch out for cabbage white caterpillars too and pick them off as necessary. If you notice a whitefly infestation, remove the lower leaves of the affected plants.

Greenhouse (if You Have One)

Continue to be mindful of watering to reduce the risk of fungal diseases. Keep an eye out for pests too, treating with biological agents as necessary.

SEPTEMBER

Soil

Feed any bare soil with a low-nutrient mulch like leaf mold, and sow green manures where you can.

Composting

Store compost that's ready to use for next year in bags and begin a new pile.

Vegetables

Most of your harvesting will be done this month, so you'll be kept busy on the vegetable patch. You'll also need to clear any diseased plants and continue to weed regularly.

Pests and Disease

Watch out for brassica whitefly, cabbage white caterpillars, and leek rust this month, treating as necessary. Slugs also tend to be at their most troublesome now, so keep setting traps as required. Bear in mind that if you're using nematodes, they'll stop being efficient as soon as the soil temperature falls below 50°F (10°C).

Greenhouse (if You Have One)

September is a tricky time for greenhouses: the days are often still warm, but the nights are cooler, so you'll need to stay on top of ventilation, keeping windows and doors open during the day and closing them at night. You'll need to water your plants less often now too. Continue to check for pests and disease, removing as necessary.

OCTOBER

Soil

It's likely that you'll now have much more bare soil, so mulch this well to improve the fertility and moisture for next year. However, avoid adding compost now, as a lot of nutrients will be lost over winter: it's best to save it for the spring. You can also add lime now, which would be a useful addition to areas where you intend to grow brassicas next year. However, remember to avoid adding lime to any area where you plan to grow potatoes.

Composting

You may find that your garden is generating a lot of waste now. If you have too much for your compost bin, make temporary stores in sacks and top up the compost bin when you can. Be sure to leave your compost covered to keep it warm. In areas of bare land, you can also add compost trenches.

Vegetables

If you're saving seeds for next year, now's the time to collect them and dry them out. You'll still be harvesting many of your crops too, but be mindful of the last frost date, and make sure you do this beforehand.

Pests and Disease

To reduce the risk of fungal diseases, be sure to remove any dead leaves from your winter brassicas. Make sure that these crops are protected by bird netting too, as pigeons are a threat over the winter.

Maintaining a Healthy Growing Area

Encourage helpful insects to spend the winter in your garden by leaving inviting leaf piles in unused corners. You could even make a stack of logs (if you have some) to provide a welcoming habitat.

Greenhouse (if You Have One)

It's time to clean the greenhouse again. You want to make sure no pests are planning to spend the winter there. Wash out all containers, and check any plant you intend to bring inside for the winter.

NOVEMBER

Soil

The soil is likely to be consistently wet again now, so avoid compaction, and make use of planks to walk on. Use mulch to cover bare areas, but don't neglect your weeding duties. Keep on collecting fallen leaves and store them in bin bags to make leaf mold.

Composting

The vast amount of waste generated by a garden at this time of year tempts many people to make bonfires, but I'd advise against this. It can destroy beneficial life in your garden and harm the biodiversity you've been working to create. Store excess waste in bags until it will fit in the compost bin. Continue to turn the compost regularly to stimulate decomposition.

Vegetables

Any remaining root crops should now be lifted and stored. Check your leeks regularly for bolting, and make sure your brassicas are netted to protect against the pigeons.

Pests and Disease

Continue to remove any dead leaves from brassica plants to deter pests and disease. Cabbage whitefly and some aphids are still a threat, so keep an eye out for these pests too, as well as leek moths and leek rust.

Greenhouse (if You Have One)

Having cleaned your greenhouse, you shouldn't have any leftover debris from the sowing season, but if you do, you'll need to remove it now to reduce the risk of pests. If you notice spiders, leave them alone: they'll help control unwelcome visitors over the winter. One extra thing I like to do around this time of year is grease the legs of my shelves with fruit tree grease. This prevents vine weevils from climbing up to lay their eggs.

❖ **Fun Fact:** For a sweeter tomato harvest, try sprinkling baking soda into the soil around your tomato plants. It decreases the soil acidity, boosting the sweetness of the fruit.

11

ADAPTING TO THE NEEDS OF YOUR CLIMATE: A GUIDE TO GROWING ZONES

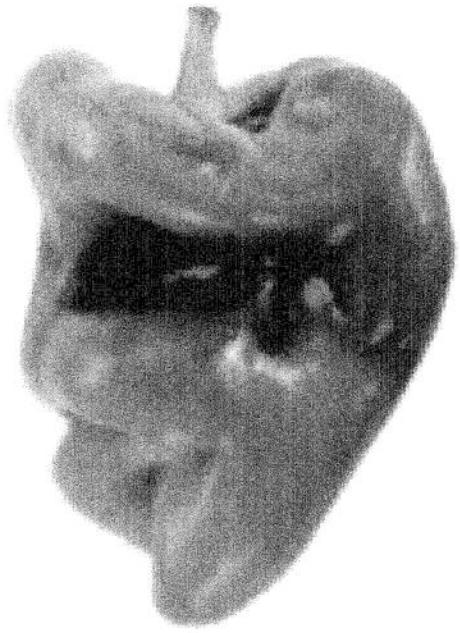

When I moved to the UK, I found the most confusing thing to get to grips with was understanding the difference in hardiness zones—and I found the same thing again when I moved back to California. Unless you're making a similar extreme move, this won't be a problem for you, but where you may run into trouble is when you're reading a guide designed for a different growing region than the one you live in. It's for this reason that it was important for me to include a chapter on different growing zones, and here I'll provide you with links to the zone maps for the UK, the USA, Australia, and Canada.

UNDERSTANDING HARDINESS ZONES

Put simply, hardiness zones help gardeners know which plants have the best chance of success in their growing area. They are marked on maps, which help you compare your climate with the ideal climate for the plants you want to grow.

The USDA zone map is color-coded by zone, and the majority of other countries, including the UK, also color-code their maps. Often seed packets mark the hardiness zone using the corresponding color, referencing which map they relate to.

Zone maps are useful, but it's important to bear in mind that they have their limitations. Plant health is affected by numerous factors including air quality, soil drainage, and humidity, and periods of extreme temperature can skew the data used to create the maps. It's also important to remember that microclimates can occur even within a single garden. Hardness maps should be used, then, as a guideline, but as you get to know your garden and its climate, you'll have a better idea of what crops are suited to your growing conditions.

CONVERTING HARDINESS ZONES

The most frequently used zone maps are the USDA Hardiness Zone map for the USA and the RHS Hardiness Zone map for the UK. However, most large countries have a version of a hardiness map. If you don't live in an area where the USDA or UK maps are appropriate, your best bet is to search online for your country's equivalent. You can also convert hardiness zones fairly easily, however.

Most guides you come across will use the USDA zone map. You can find out what corresponds with this map with a little bit of simple math. Calculate the lowest average temperature of the area you're interested in, and add 10 degrees for every higher zone. The average temperature of USDA Zone 11 is 40°F (4°C), so if you live in an area where this is the lowest average thermometer reading, this is the zone that applies to you. USDA Zone 12 is 50°F (10°C), and each zone continues in increments of 10 degrees.

HOW ZONE MAPS ARE CREATED

We won't go into too much detail on this, but I find a small amount of background information helps to understand what it is we're looking at.

The USDA zone map was created by the US Department of Agriculture to give a clear idea of which plants will thrive in specific climates. Zones are separated at every 10 degrees and show which plants will survive the lowest temperatures in each region. The zones go from Zone 1 to Zone 13, with 1 being the coolest and 13 being the warmest. When there is a variation within a single zone, subzones are indicated with the letters "a" or "b."

The map was created based on the average minimum temperature over a 30-year period, which means it's relatively accurate. By using the lowest (rather than the highest) temperature, the maps show the hazards of freezing conditions for each plant. They are updated regularly to reflect climate change.

QUICK ACCESS TO COMMON ZONE MAPS

Most countries have a hardiness zone map of sorts, so if you live somewhere not covered by these four maps, search online for your local data or make a conversion based on the USDA map. However, for quick reference, here are links to the maps you're most likely to be using.

USDA Zone Map: https://planthardiness.ars.usda.gov/
UK Zone Map: https://ebps.org.uk/no-parent-pages/uk-hardiness-zones/
Australia Zone Map:
http://www.bom.gov.au/jsp/ncc/climate_aver-

ages/temperature/index.jsp?maptype=3&period=an#maps

Canada Zone Map: http://planthardiness.gc.ca/images/PHZ_2014_CFS_Map_30M.pdf

❖ **Fun Fact:** On average, the global temperature increased from 33.08°F (0.6°C) to 33.8°F (1°C) over the 20th century.

LEAVE A 1-CLICK REVIEW

I would be incredibly grateful if you could take 60 seconds to write a brief review on Amazon, even if it is just a few sentences!

CONCLUSION

No book will ever completely prepare you for every challenge you may face in the garden—and if it could, where would the excitement be? Every gardener's journey is personal. There will be highs, and there will be lows, but one thing I can tell you for sure is that I don't know one single person who's gone back to conventional gardening after trying it the organic way. If you're under the misconception that organic gardening simply means not using chemicals, you're bound to be disappointed and doubt the strength of this method, but as soon as you realize that an organic garden, when nurtured properly, supports itself and counteracts its own problems, it's impossible not to see the benefits.

As long as you live by the five building blocks of organic gardening we discussed in Chapter 1, you're bound to see more and more success with every year that you tend your garden.

There's always more to learn—and you will learn it as you grow—but you now have the fundamental knowledge required to start a thriving organic vegetable gardening. All that's left for you to do is to get outside and use it.

I would like to ask one thing of you before you do, however. My mission here is to squash the misconceptions about organic gardening and show even the most skeptical of gardeners how effective it is… and to do that, I need as many people to read this guide as possible. Therefore, it would be extremely helpful if you could leave a review on Amazon—this is what will help other gardeners find the resources they need for organic gardening success.

Let's dispel this idea that chemicals are needed to grow vegetables. It doesn't make sense, and it's harming our health and the environment.

Now, get out there and start nurturing that soil!

And don't forget to Join the Organic Gardeners Club Facebook Group, just scan the QR code below with your phone

REFERENCES

10 Fascinating Facts, Figures and Traditions Around Harvest Time. (2016, September 14). Bannisters Yorkshire Family Farm. https://www.bannistersfarm.co.uk/blog/10-fascinating-facts-figures-and-traditions-aro und-harvest-time/

11 Things You Might Not Know About Organic Farming. (2016, May 27).

www.mentalfloss.com.

https://www.mentalfloss.com/article/80655/11-things-you-might-not-know-about-organ

ic-farming

Almanac, O. F. (2021a, January 6). *Starting Seeds Indoors: How and When to Start*

Seeds. Old Farmer's Almanac.

https://www.almanac.com/starting-seeds-indoors-how-and-when-start-seeds

Almanac, O. F. (2021b, April 3). *Tips for Transplanting Seedlings*. Old Farmer's

Almanac. https://www.almanac.com/tips-transplanting-seedlings

Australian Government Bureau of Meteorology. (2016, November). *Australian*

Climate Averages—Maximum, Minimum & Mean Temperature maps.

www.bom.gov.au.

http://www.bom.gov.au/jsp/ncc/climate_averages/temperature/index.jsp?maptype=3&

period=an#maps

Bardin, J. (2012, June 30). *Why Supermarket Tomatoes Tend to Taste Bland*. Los

Angeles Times.

https://www.latimes.com/nation/la-xpm-2012-jun-30-la-sci-tomato-taste-20120630-sto

ry.html

Bayliss, M. (2018, January 30). *15 Essential Gardening Tools for Small Organic*

Gardens. Gardeners' Magazine.

https://gardenersmag.com/gardening-tool-for-small-organic-gardens/

BioExpedition Publishing. (2017). *Facts about Snails—Snail Facts and Information.*

Snail-World.com. https://www.snail-world.com/snail-facts/

Brian Clark Howard. (2018, March 21). *How to Start an Organic Garden in 9 Easy Steps*. Good Housekeeping; Good Housekeeping. https://www.goodhousekeeping.-com/home/gardening/advice/g2104/organic-gardenin g-tips-460309/

British Pteridological Society. (n.d.). *UK Hardiness Zones.* The British Pteridological

Society. Retrieved July 19, 2021, from

https://ebps.org.uk/no-parent-pages/uk-hardiness-zones/

Castle, S. (2020, January 2). *10 Tools You Need to Tend Your Organic Vegetable*

Garden. Food & Wine.

https://www.foodandwine.com/how/top-organic-products-tools-home-garden

Collins, C. (n.d.). *Principles of Organic Gardening | Garden Organic.*

www.gardenorganic.org.uk. https://www.gardenorganic.org.uk/principles

Dermer, L. (2014, March 9). *How to Sprout Sweet Potatoes for Slips — Green*

Shoots for Planting | Southern Exposure Seed Exchange. Southern Exposure Seed

Exchange.

https://blog.southernexposure.com/2014/03/how-to-sprout-sweet-potatoes-for-slips-g

reen-shoots-for-planting/

Duford, M. J. (n.d.). *What Is Organic Gardening? (And Why Is It Important?).* Home for the Harvest. Retrieved July 19, 2021, from https://www.homefortheharvest.com/what-is-organic-gardening/

Dyer, M. H. (2021, January 30). *Hardiness Zones in Britain—USDA and RHS Hardiness Zones.* www.gardeningknowhow.com. https://www.gardeningknowhow.com/planting-zones/uk-hardiness-zones.htm Espiritu, K. (2017, April 3). *5 Best Seed Starting Mixes For Explosive Plant Growth.* Epic Gardening. https://www.epicgardening.com/best-seed-starting-mix/ *Everything you need to know about the Hori Hori knife.* (2018, July 5). www.japeto.co.uk. https://www.japeto.co.uk/blog/27/2/what-is-a-hori-

hori-knife *Garden Organic.* (n.d.). www.gardenorganic.org.uk. Retrieved July 19, 2021, from https://www.gardenorganic.org.uk/planning%20your%20planting

Garden Trivia & Facts. (n.d.). www.yates.com.au. Retrieved July 19, 2021, from https://www.yates.com.au/ideas-plans/project-guides-articles/all/garden-trivia/ Grant, B. L. (2021, April 28). *Hardiness Zone Converter: Information On Hardiness Zones Outside U.S.* www.gardeningknowhow.com. https://www.gardeningknowhow.com/planting-zones/hardiness-zone-converter.htm *Grow Easy: 15 Foolproof Plants for Organic Gardens.* (2009, April 6). WebEcoist. https://webecoist.momtastic.-com/2009/04/06/grow-easy-15-foolproof-plants-for-organ ic-gardens/

Hardiness Zones Explained. (n.d.). PRO-MIX Gardening. Retrieved July 19, 2021, from https://www.promixgardening.com/en/tips/hardiness-zones-explained-78

Harvesting and storage | Garden Organic. (n.d.). www.gardenorganic.org.uk.

Retrieved July 19, 2021, from

https://www.gardenorganic.org.uk/harvesting-and-storage

Holman, J. (2011, May 20). *Five of the Best...Natural and Organic Fertilisers.*

Theecologist.org.

https://theecologist.org/2011/may/20/five-bestnatural-and-organic-fertilisers

Home Composting | Garden Organic. (n.d.). www.gardenorganic.org.uk. Retrieved

July 19, 2021, from https://www.gardenorganic.org.uk/compost

How to Grow Organic Mushrooms. (2021, June 14). WikiHow.

https://www.wikihow.com/Grow-Organic-Mushrooms

How to Make Soil More Acidic Organically | Kellogg Garden Organics™. (n.d.).

www.kellogggarden.com.

https://www.kellogggarden.com/blog/soil/how-to-make-soil-more-acidic-organically/

J. I. Rodale. (2021, June 11). Wikipedia. https://en.wikipedia.org/wiki/J._I._Rodale

McMahon, M. (n.d.). *What is a Soil Thermometer? (with pictures). Home Questions*

Answered. Retrieved July 19, 2021, from

https://www.homequestionsanswered.com/what-is-a-soil-thermometer.htm

Minister of Natural Resources Canada. (2014). *Fort McMurray EDMONTON Calgary*

Vancouver VICTORIA.

http://planthardiness.gc.ca/
images/PHZ_2014_CFS_Map_30M.pdf

Organic Gardening. (n.d.). www.rhs.org.uk. Retrieved July 19, 2021, from https://www.rhs.org.uk/advice/profile?pid=822

Organic Weed Management | Garden Organic. (n.d.). www.-gardenorganic.org.uk. Retrieved July 19, 2021, from https://www.gardenorganic.org.uk/weed-management
Pests and Diseases | Garden Organic. (n.d.). www.gardenorganic.org.uk. Retrieved July 19, 2021, from https://www.gardenorganic.org.uk/pests-and-diseases

Price, M. (2021, March 4). *Why Knowing Your USDA Hardiness Zone Is Crucial for*

Keeping Plants Alive. CNET.

https://www.cnet.com/home/yard-and-outdoors/what-is-hardiness-zone-map-us-usda/

Rinkesh. (2016, December 25). *What is Organic Food and 15 Health Benefits of*

Eating Organic Food. Conserve Energy Future.

https://www.conserve-energy-future.com/15-health-benefits-eating-organic-food.php

Rinkesh. (2017, January 5). *35 Facts About Climate Change.* Conserve Energy

Future.

https://www.conserve-energy-future.com/various-climate-change-facts-php.php

Sansone Arricca. (2021, February 12). *An Array of Organic Fertilizer Options for Your Plants.* Treehugger. https://www.treehugger.com/best-organic-fertilizers-5078293 *Seed: Sowing Outdoors.* (n.d.). www.rhs.org.uk. Retrieved July 19, 2021, from https://www.rhs.org.uk/advice/profile?pid=206

TIMG, A. (2020, February 12). *How To Understand Growing Zones & Hardiness Maps to Plant Smart.* This Is My Garden. https://thisismygarden.com/2020/02/understand-growing-zones/

Tong, C. (n.d.). *Harvesting and Storing Home Garden Vegetables.* Extension.umn.edu. Retrieved July 19, 2021, from https://extension.umn.edu/planting-and-growing-guides/harvesting-and-storing-home-garden-vegetables

Topsoil: Buying. (n.d.). www.rhs.org.uk. Retrieved July 19, 2021, from https://www.rhs.org.uk/advice/profile?pid=375

Uitert, M. van. (2018, January 4). *13 Organic Gardening Supplies Every Woman Needs.* Pampered Chicken Mama:

Raising Backyard Chickens. https://thefrugalchicken.com/organic-gardening-supplies/

USDA. (2020). *USDA Plant Hardiness Zone Map*. Usda.gov.

https://planthardiness.ars.usda.gov/

Vegetables All Year Round | www.gardenorganic.org.uk. (2017). Gardenorganic.org.uk. https://www.gardenorganic.org.uk/vegetables-all-year-round Vinje, E. (2012a, December 7). *How to Grow Garlic Organically*. Planet Natural. https://www.planetnatural.com/growing-garlic/

Vinje, E. (2012b, December 8). *Beginner Tomato Gardening Guide*. Planet Natural. https://www.planetnatural.com/tomato-gardening/

Vinje, E. (2012c, December 8). *How to Grow Carrots Organically*. Planet Natural. https://www.planetnatural.com/growing-carrots/

Vinje, E. (2012d, December 8). *How To Grow Fennel Organically*. Planet Natural. https://www.planetnatural.com/growing-fennel/

Vinje, E. (2012e, December 8). *How to Grow Peppers Organically*. Planet Natural. https://www.planetnatural.com/growing-peppers/

Vinje, E. (2012f, December 8). *How to Grow Pumpkins Organically*. Planet Natural. https://www.planetnatural.com/growing-pumpkins/

Vinje, E. (2012g, December 8). *How to Grow Radishes Organically*. Planet Natural. https://www.planetnatural.com/growing-radish/

Vinje, E. (2012h, December 8). *How to Grow Rhubarb Organically*. Planet Natural. https://www.planetnatural.com/growing-rhubarb/

Vinje, E. (2012i, December 8). *How to Grow Squash Organically*. Planet Natural. https://www.planetnatural.com/growing-squash/

Vinje, E. (2012j, December 8). *How to Grow Sweet Potatoes Organically*. Planet

Natural. https://www.planetnatural.com/growing-sweet-potatoes/

Webmaster. (2021, June 3). *24 Fun Facts About Gardening and Plants—Garden*

Simply. Gardensimply.com.

https://gardensimply.com/fun-facts-about-gardening-and-plants

Why Grow Organic? (n.d.). Organic Growers School. https://organicgrowersschool.org/gardeners/library/why-grow-organic/

Your Organic Garden in April | Garden Organic. (n.d.). www.-gardenorganic.org.uk.

Retrieved July 19, 2021, from

https://www.gardenorganic.org.uk/your-organic-garden-april

Your Organic Garden in August | Garden Organic. (n.d.). www.gardenorganic.org.uk.

Retrieved July 19, 2021, from

https://www.gardenorganic.org.uk/your-organic-garden-august

Your Organic Garden in December and January | Garden Organic. (n.d.). www.gardenorganic.org.uk. Retrieved July 19, 2021, from https://www.gardenorganic.org.uk/your-organic-garden-december-and-january *Your Organic Garden in February | Garden Organic*. (n.d.). www.gardenorganic.org.uk. Retrieved July 19, 2021, from https://www.gardenorganic.org.uk/What-to-do-in-February

Your Organic Garden in July | Garden Organic. (n.d.). www.-gardenorganic.org.uk. Retrieved July 19, 2021, from https://www.gardenorganic.org.uk/node/1342

Your Organic Garden in June | Garden Organic. (n.d.). www.-gardenorganic.org.uk.

Retrieved July 19, 2021, from

https://www.gardenorganic.org.uk/your-organic-garden-june

Your Organic Garden in March | Garden Organic. (n.d.). www.gardenorganic.org.uk.

Retrieved July 19, 2021, from https://www.gardenorganic.org.uk/what-do-march

Your Organic Garden in May | Garden Organic. (n.d.). www.-gardenorganic.org.uk.

Retrieved July 19, 2021, from

https://www.gardenorganic.org.uk/your-organic-garden-may

Your Organic Garden in November | Garden Organic. (n.d.). www.gardenorganic.org.uk. Retrieved July 19, 2021, from https://www.gardenorganic.org.uk/your-organic-garden-november *Your Organic Garden in October | Garden Organic*. (n.d.). www.gardenorganic.org.uk. Retrieved July 19, 2021, from https://www.gardenorganic.org.uk/your-organic-garden-october *Your Organic Garden in September | Garden Organic*. (n.d.). www.gardenorganic.org.uk. Retrieved July 19, 2021, from https://www.gardenorganic.org.uk/your-organic-garden-september

Printed in Great Britain
by Amazon

74875467R00106